BIG
BUG
CREEK

Michael Hawkins

STORIES OF GROWING ARIZONA

BIG
BUG
CREEK

For information about this title, contact the publisher:

PH&A, Inc.
phyllis@designphar.com
www.designphar.com

ISBNs:

979-8-9915037-0-9 (softcover)
979-8-9915037-1-6 (eBook)

Printed in the United States of America

Cover and Interior design: 1106 Design
Front and Back Cover Photography: By Abagail T Polito

For

William Henry Perry & Mary Agnes Clark Perry
and all the Perrys that follow

TABLE OF CONTENTS

ACKNOWLEDGMENTS

Many of these stories could not have been written without the treasure trove of family history left by my maternal grandmother, Maud Perry Daly. An English and Latin teacher, she loved to read and write and to share the product with friends and loved ones.

Geraldine Haase and Barbara Gronemann engaged in a detailed ancestral study, "The William Henry Perry Family" (November 2009), done in connection with the Friends of the Agua Fria Monument, a nonprofit celebrating President Clinton's designation of the Agua Fria National Monument, which includes the Perry homestead. On the drive north on I-17 from Phoenix to Flagstaff, the Sunset Point rest stop will be on the left. To the right is a flat expanse of land, a tabletop landmark. That is Perry Mesa.

My brother Barry, the oldest of the Perry grandchildren, who shared many of these memories. Laura Ferguson, my faithful assistant and a world-class proofreader, was instrumental in putting this collection together.

Nothing in life for me would be possible without the counsel, advice, and constructive criticism of my wife, Phyllis, who is particularly valuable because she shared many of the experiences described in the stories that follow.

PERRY INTRODUCTION

The stories that follow involve members of my mother's family, the Perrys, who migrated to central Arizona in the 1870s. The patriarch, William Henry Perry (1844–1929), was an adventuresome young man from Holyoke, Massachusetts. The family was well enough off for William Henry and his father to make the months-long trip from Boston to San Francisco with dreams of taking part in the California Gold Rush. Just getting to California was no easy task. The Panama Canal was a half-century away from creation, so the voyage involved sailing around the tip of South America, navigating the waters south of Tierra del Fuego, and then "taking ship" for the five-thousand-mile voyage to California.

On one of his trips home, William Henry met Mary Agnes Clark (1850–1915). A young Irish lass with sparkling black eyes, Mary was working as a governess for a neighboring family. How she got to America, no less adventuresome than William Henry's California forays, is recounted in "Native Daughter," the story that follows.

Following a brief courtship, William Henry Perry and Mary Agnes Clark were married. The first of what would be nine children was Henry Jones (1874–1948). At eighteen months, he would sail down to Panama with his mother, then travel by train across the Isthmus and again by ship to California to join William Henry, who was now back to chasing dreams of gold. When the gold did not pan out, the family turned to raising sheep along the banks of the Kern River,

1

near what is now Bakersfield. The wanderlust struck again and, with a herd of three thousand sheep, the family headed south—through central California, across the tip of Nevada, and into central Arizona after crossing the Colorado River at Lee's Ferry.

The Perrys settled near the banks of the Agua Fria River, near its Ash Creek tributary and up against the sometimes-dry Big Bug Creek. The nearest town, if it could be called that, was Cordes, a hardy outpost of some twenty people. The nearest community of any size was Prescott, the territorial capital, fifty miles away and, according to the census of the day, consisting of less than two thousand citizens. The entire Arizona Territory, from the Grand Canyon to the Sonoran border, had less than fifty thousand.

Eight children—six girls and two boys—would follow, born either at the family ranch house or at Johnny Osborn Springs near the San Francisco Peaks, where the sheep would be moved north in the summer. Charlotte Elizabeth (1876–1958) was the oldest of those born in Arizona; Eben Prescott (1892–1962) was the youngest. In between were Mary Adeline (1878–1903), Grace (1881–1963), William Kittredge (1883–1954), Mabel (1885–1956), Maud (1887–1973), and Agnes (1890–1924). The family eventually moved to the Phoenix area and turned to dairy and cotton farming. In some of the stories that follow, William Henry (the old man), his son William Kittredge, and two of the daughters, Mabel and Maud, figure prominently. A full listing of the Perry children and a brief biography of each appear in the addendum to this collection.

Pen-and-ink sketch of the William K. Perry ranch on the Agua Fria River three miles east of Cordes Junction, Arizona. This is a sketch made by Homer Redden, husband of Lottie Perry during a visit in the late 1890s. The Perry family lived and grew up on the ranch until 1901 when William K. Perry moved to a farm on the Salt River near Phoenix, Arizona.

NATIVE DAUGHTER

S he was born before the advent of the automobile, before the widespread availability of electricity, yet she was the model of a modern woman. She grew up in what today we would certainly describe as poverty—the earliest photographs show her standing in front of a sod house, in rugged clothing with that gaunt look we now associate with third-world countries—yet she enjoyed a life of incredible riches. In her younger years, her home contained few books other than the King James version of the Bible, yet she became incredibly literate, eventually writing a master's thesis on Shakespeare's concept of loyalty.

She grew up when Native Americans were not consigned to reservations and lived to see men walk on the moon, but she was largely unimpressed by the material advances of modern society. She was Maud Perry Daly. Pioneer Arizonan, Latin scholar, a divorced single parent when that was unheard of, a teacher who ran a classroom with the discipline of a Marine drill instructor without ever raising a hand in anger, my mother's mother who seldom heard the word "Grandmother." She was simply Gammo.

It is hard to imagine the Arizona of her youth. The Civil War had ended less than twenty years earlier. Statehood was twenty years in the future. There was not a single mile of paved highway anywhere. Mining, farming, and ranching were the predominant industries. Prescott was the territorial capital, a bustling city of ten thousand hardy souls. The mining communities to the east—Dewey, Humboldt, Mayer, and Cordes—were alive with fortune seekers. Their saloons roared to life at night with all sorts of mischief available to those so inclined. Phoenix was a three-day wagon trip away and a place to be avoided in July and August, with not even an electric fan to relieve the desert heat.

Her parents had come from Massachusetts by way of California. William Henry Perry, her father, was from Lynn and later Fitchburg, small manufacturing and farming communities in the rural part of the Commonwealth. His forebears had come to colonial America from seventeenth-century England to escape religious persecution, break free of the class system, and make a great fortune, which they never really found. They infused their son with a sense of independence and adventure, the notion that a better life was to be found somewhere else, if only you were willing to go there. At the age of nine, his father took him to California for the Gold Rush, sailing around Cape Horn, through the fearsome Tierra del Fuego straits.

Gammo's mother, Mary Agnes Clark Perry, was an Irish immigrant. Born in Dublin, her father was an officer in the occupying British Army. Shortly after her birth, he sold his commission, left the family for America, and was never heard from again. Her mother passed away when she was nine, leaving her in the care of her grandmother, who in turn died two years later. The landlady in the building where they lived took over, only to pass away herself. This left Mary Agnes to live in a Dublin convent, paid for by a modest inheritance. When she was sixteen, the nuns turned her out with the equivalent of several hundred dollars, which she used to book passage to Boston, encouraged by letters from a former convent mate who had made the passage earlier.

After the thirty-day passage to the New World, Mary Agnes arrived in Boston and was met by her friend, Mamie Kelly, from convent days, with whom she lived until she found work as a governess for a local family, who were friends and neighbors of William Kittredge Perry and Charlotte Jones (Prescott) Perry, William Henry's parents. On one of his trips back from California, he met a governess working for a neighbor family. He was, according to Gammo's notes written in the 1950s, "A handsome young rascal, with dancing black eyes, good clothes and a team of matched horses."

The courtship was brief. They were young—he was twenty-nine, she twenty-four—and they had their lives, perhaps more challenging and eventful than they ever imagined, ahead of them. They would have nine children, the first being Henry Jones, born in Massachusetts, who would soon accompany his mother on the long trek to California. William Henry would meet his son for the first time on their arrival in San Francisco.

After gold mining did not pan out, William Henry and a friend, William Helm, established a ranch near Bakersfield on the banks of the Kern River. Family lore has it that a substantial oil deposit was later discovered on the property, but William Henry didn't wait around for it. Displaying the impatience and wanderlust that by this time was very much part of him, he stayed around only long enough to build up a herd of some three thousand sheep and acquire several wagons and horses to pull them. In the fall of 1875, he convinced his partner, Helm, to head south to Arizona.

This was no day trip. To get there, they would have to travel 1,200 miles, crossing the Mohave Desert and parts of Nevada and Utah in the process. They crossed the Utah-Arizona border at House Rock Valley on a trail known as the Mormon Road, which led across the Paris Plateau and down the Vermillion Cliffs. Then their biggest obstacle presented itself as they arrived at the banks of the mighty Colorado River. The Navajo word for this point translates as "where the boat sits." Major John Wesley Powell, the famed Grand Canyon explorer, had given one of his boats to John Doyle Lee, who established a ferrying business for those wishing to cross. Thus, the name Lee's Ferry, as it is known to this day. Gammo sets the scene:

The supplies and wagons were ferried across; the Sheep had to swim. This they refused to until Mrs. Perry stood on the far bank with a pail of barley and called Billy, the lead ram who was her pet. He plunged in with the herd close behind. Many Sheep perished in the turbulent Colorado.

There is really no way to know if they even knew where they were going. The trail took them south, along the Echo Cliffs, to the Little Colorado River. Their route paralleled what is now Highway 89, crossing the Moenkopi and Dinnebeto Washes. Crossing the Little Colorado near Tuba City, they headed south toward the San Francisco Peaks, past Chalender, then south along Sycamore Creek. In the spring of 1876, they reached Badger Springs about four miles southeast of Prescott. This became home. In the summer, they would drive the sheep north to Johnny Osborne's Spring, where Charlotte Elizabeth was born, the first of the Arizona children. Mary Adeline was born on one of the return trips to Badger Springs.

Eventually, they would homestead land about three miles east of what is now Cordes Junction, near the mouth of Little Ash Creek and the Agua Fria River and up against the sometimes-dry Big Bug Creek. It was no Eden, but there was plenty of land and water and the climate was relatively mild. Several more Perry children were born there: William Kittredge, Mable, Agnes, Maud (Gammo), Grace, and Eben. Charlotte, known as Lottie, was the eldest.

Henry Jones was born in Fitchburg, Massachusetts, his mother having returned there for the purpose of his birth. At ten months, Jones, as everyone called him, and his mother sailed from Boston to Panama, where they crossed the Isthmus by train and then, to quote Gammo, "took ship again for San Francisco." Young Jones's travels were not over. He could not have been more than two years old when the Perrys and their sheep headed to Arizona.

It was a hard life in their new home, but the Perrys made do. To outsiders, it must have seemed an isolated and lonely existence. Isolated it was, but hardly uneventful as Gammo recalls:

Visitors often commented on the lonesome life of the Perry family, but to them it was the most wonderful existence in the world. They desired not outside companionship. They knew the natural world intimately and Nature withheld no secret from their prying eyes and busy minds. There were the best of horses, and the boys and girls rode like centaurs, astride in the world of side-saddles or bareback like Indians. They had an endless array of pets. They went on picnics. They danced until the sun rose. There were a constant stream of visitors to the ranch house. They played the organ, the violin, the banjo. They prospected for gold or made collections of bird eggs from the tiny white pellet of the hummingbird to the big speckled oval of the kildee. They played, quarreled, worked and loved together. From parental guidance and necessary work they learned discipline, self-reliance, and honesty. An inherited sense of humor produced endless jokes and laughter.

There was no school anywhere near the ranch home. A visitor, a college man from back East, suggested his younger brother, Walter Hastings, as a tutor. He had wanted to come West, and this was his chance. He ran a tight ship, facing few of the problems teachers see today. His results were nothing short of spectacular: Every Perry went on to college, and many became teachers themselves. When a district school opened at Cordes in 1888, the Perry children were among its best students.

When it came time for college, even getting the children there proved quite a chore. Because the Tempe Normal School (now Arizona State University) had no living arrangements for students, a modest home was purchased in Tempe in 1896 to avoid moving the children back and forth. Five years later, the ranch, including the livestock and brand, was sold, and the family moved to the Phoenix area. Gammo entered college there in 1902. She was an active and engaged student, serving as the first editor of the school paper (now the *State Press*). She graduated with honors, receiving the coveted Harvard Prize in 1906. The school was contained in one building, now called Old Main. Today, on its second floor is the Perry Conference Room in honor of Willam Henry and Mary Agnes Perry, established by three Perry grandchildren.

She began teaching in 1910 and for years was a mainstay in an organization of Statehood Teachers. She taught until 1958. For a large portion of her teaching career, she was at Chandler High School, where she taught English and Latin. Latin, in particular, had a structure and order to it, and she would pound it in like math tables. I, for one, was afraid not to learn it. She was very tough if you got it wrong. Her students included future lawyers and judges, including Ray Haire, who went on to serve on the Arizona Court of Appeals, and grocer Eddie Basha, easily one of Arizona's greatest public citizens. I would spend summers with her in Chandler. Invariably we would run into her former students. Their comments were strikingly similar: "You were a great teacher, Mrs. Daly. You were tough and demanding, but a great friend. Thank you for having been there."

In her later years, she returned to the vicinity of her youth, living for a time in Mayer, in a trailer park, beneath an old smokestack, a reminder of mining days gone by. She later moved to Prescott and lived in a mobile home park near her brother Eben and his wife Tilly, the sister of famed World War I pilot Frank Luke. When Eben passed away, she moved to the Hassayampa Inn. We encouraged her to go to the Pioneers' Home. She was clearly eligible, but too independent. She wanted her own time and space.

When I returned from the Marine Corps in 1973, my mother told me Gammo was near the end of her time. Phyllis, her great-grandson

Aaron, and I drove to see her in Sedona. We reminisced about the changes in life in Arizona over the span of her years. She told me of a Native American friend she knew at the district school in Cordes and how they had talked about the difference in the approaches different cultures take toward the end of life. "Why," the friend wondered, "do your people dwell on the last moments of life? Why not celebrate the moments of joy, the good times?" She reached out to me with one of her once-strong hands, now frail and brittle. "Promise me something," she said. "When I am gone, think of me for just a little while, of the wonderful times we had together, and then turn your thoughts and energy to the living, to your children. They will need you. I will not."

There was one last letter. A thank-you note, really. The same bold handwriting, the Latin phrases at the bottom. And then she was gone. A few years short of a full century. She touched many lives, many for the better for it. On a windy spring day in 1974, we put her to rest in the Double Butte Cemetery in Tempe. Next to her mother, near her brothers and sisters. There is an order to all this, I thought. She sprang from the soil of Arizona, and now she goes back to it.

THE PEOPLE
v. UNCLE WINNIE

The uncle in this story, like the grandfather in "The Search for Effie Dee," was someone I never met. He married my grandmother's sister Mabel one year after the events described in the following story. They had met when her father took her to a community dance in Mayer, near the Perry family ranch on the Agua Fria River near Cordes, both small communities in rural Arizona Territory. He appears, stern and serious, in a 1921 photo of the Perry family at a gathering that has become known as the Perry Picnic, an event that carries on to this day.

He was Henry Vincent Rosenberger, an unlikely cowboy, whose Mennonite faith had forced his family to flee religious persecution in Germany. Landing first in Kansas, the family moved to Arizona Territory at the turn of the twentieth century, settling in the Dewey-Valverde area. Vincent (he never apparently used his first name) was in his mid-twenties. His mother, bearing the tongue of her Central European childhood, had trouble pronouncing the letter "V," so she referred to her son as "Winnie." The name stuck.[1]

Winnie, a strapping young man with a ready smile, was working as a hand at the Fort Rock Ranch when a job opportunity presented itself, this time not just as a ranch hand, but one with management responsibilities. The Windmill Ranch, located in the upper reaches of Yavapai County, eighteen miles northeast of Jerome and above the Mogollon Rim, was undergoing a change in management. The new owners, William Cox and Pat Hurley, operating under the name D.K. Cattle Company, had purchased the ranch from James Black, known to all as James the elder, an early cattleman from Flagstaff. As a condition of Winnie's hiring, Cox and Hurley wanted the old ranch crew replaced.

Those to be let go included Peter Paul "Rock" Hochderffer, scion of a pioneer Flagstaff family. Winnie was the choice to be the new foreman.

It thus fell to Winnie to discharge Hochderffer and his sidekicks, which he did on February 21, 1907. That evening, Winnie, Rock, and others rode into Jerome to attend the Fireman's dance.[2] While there, Winnie and Rock had dinner together. Rock took the opportunity to air his grievances about his discharge. Winnie, who was simply carrying out the wishes of the owners, did not take well to the criticism. Underlying the tension between the two were persistent rumors spreading among cattlemen at the time that the D.K. outfit did not "confine its brand to its own stock"—a refined way of accusing them of cattle rustling. Rock Hochderffer was thought to be one of the sources of these rumors.[3]

Two days after Hochderffer's dismissal, Winnie and Ernest Cox were at the Windmill Ranch when Rock and several of the other former ranch hands rode up. They had returned to gather up their belongings, intending to leave the next morning. The group had dinner that evening, after which Winnie, Cox, and others played some cards. Before the group retired for the evening, Hochderffer made a remark—that there were now some "knockers" in town. Whether good-natured ribbing or something else, Winnie took offense to the comment.

The next morning, when they were in the ranch kitchen together, Winnie told Rock that he would have to leave. The two exchanged words, which quickly turned violent. There were at least five other people at the ranch that morning. Some were Hochderffer's friends; others were affiliated in one way or another with the D.K. outfit.

While some saw the verbal confrontation between the pair, none of them actually witnessed the full sequence of events that culminated in Winnie firing his 30-30 rifle at Rock Hochderffer, mortally wounding him.[4]

Some reports have it that Jim Bailey, a part-time U.S. Forest Service ranger who was at the ranch that day, arrested Winnie on the spot. At some point, however, Winnie rode to Jerome and turned himself in to the town marshal. The following day, Winnie attended and testified at the coroner's inquest, which took place back at the Windmill Ranch. After hearing the testimony of those present at the ranch that day (including Winnie), the coroner's jury found that Winnie had acted in self-defense and that the shooting was justified.

The conclusions of the coroner's jury did not sit well with the Hochderffer family. They were convinced Rock's death had been anything but justified. In his autobiography, older brother George described what the family thought had happened:

> My younger brother, Peter Paul (Rock) Hochderffer, in the early morning of February 22, 1907, came to his death by a rifle bullet in the back, which severed the vertebrae of his spinal column. Rock, on his way home from Jerome, stopped by the Windmill headquarters of the D.K. Ranch, where Winnie Rosenberger, offended at a good-natured teasing by Rock the evening before, took revenge by shooting Rock in the back as Rock was passing through a door from one room to the other.[5]

The Hochderffers and their supporters were not about to let matters rest. As the Flagstaff hometown newspaper reported five days after the shooting:

> The matter of the killing will not be allowed rest with the verdict of the coroner's jury but the matter will be taken up

by the relatives and friends of young Hochderffer and the case will be fully investigated by the authorities of Yavapai County where the killing took place, and a warrant obtained for the arrest of Rosenberger who was handy with his gun.[6]

Family members met with Coconino County Attorney Henry Ashurst, who urged Yavapai County District Attorney Robert E. Morrison to look deeper into the matter. The efforts did not go unrewarded. A grand jury was convened, which, on May 7, 1907, charged Winnie with Rock Hochderffer's murder.[7] Winnie surrendered to authorities and was released on a $15,000 cash bond posted by Jerome merchants William C. Miller and Charles H. Hooker. Jury trial on the charges was set for May 14, 1907.

The trial, later described by the *Frontier Times* as "one of the most sensational since the Graham-Tewksbury feud some twenty years earlier,"[8] would be presided over by Richard Elihu Sloan, a justice on the Arizona Territorial Supreme Court, sitting as a trial judge on circuit. No stranger to serious trials,[9] Sloan, who would go on to become Arizona's last territorial governor and a critical figure in the struggle for statehood, had a reputation as a fair-minded jurist who ran a tight courtroom. The trial began as scheduled, less than three months after the fatal confrontation at the Windmill Ranch. Winnie Rosenberger appeared with Reese M. Ling of Prescott, a former district attorney for Yavapai County, as his defense counsel.

District Attorney Morrison acted as the prosecutor, and his first witness was Jim Bailey. Bailey had been in the room where the shooting occurred and heard the verbal confrontation between the pair. Bailey described Rosenberger as being in the kitchen when Hochderffer entered and saying to Rock: "You haven't treated me with respect, and you'll have to leave." Asked if he intended to leave, Hochderffer replied: "I don't know if I will or not." According to Bailey, Winnie replied: "You will if I get my gun." Bailey heard Hochderffer respond: "Not if I get mine first."

When Bailey saw both men start for their guns, he ran out the front door. Looking back, he saw Rosenberger get his rifle, bring it to a firing position at his waist, and pull the trigger, and he heard Hochderffer yell. When he returned to the kitchen, Bailey found Hochderffer lying face down and mortally wounded. Examining Rock's body, Bailey observed a back wound.[10] On cross-examination, Bailey admitted that when he last saw Hochderffer, Rock was reaching up toward a shelf where his pistol was located.

James L. Black, a seventeen-year-old cowboy and son of the former owner of the ranch, who testified at the earlier inquest, also told of the events leading up to the shooting.[11] The evening before, when Rosenberger and Ernest Cox were playing cards, he overheard Hochderffer make some disparaging remarks that were apparently aimed at Rosenberger. While he was getting dressed the next morning, he heard Rosenberger say to Cox that Hochderffer would have to leave the ranch that morning. When Cox told Rosenberger that Hochderffer would be coming around that morning, Rosenberger replied: "If he wants me to, I'll show him this morning." When Hochderffer came in the kitchen just after this, Black went out the kitchen window, hearing a shot as he did so.

Rock Hochderffer's friend George Peterson was next to testify. He lost his job at the Windmill when Rock was discharged.[12] The pair had been together in Jerome the night before and rode to the Windmill Ranch the next morning. Peterson and Hochderffer had slept in the ranch house outside the kitchen. Before retiring for the night, Peterson saw Hochderffer take off his gun and scabbard[13] and place them on a shelf in the room next to the kitchen. Hochderffer got up before him the next morning and left while Petersen was still dressing. He then heard something that sounded like a dish breaking. As he entered the kitchen he saw Rosenberger with a 30-30 rifle, cocked in his hand. After determining that Peterson did not have a gun with him, Rosenberger said: "I've hurt your friend, but I have nothing against you." When he approached Hochderffer's body,

Rosenberger said: "He's got a six-shooter around there; look for it." Peterson saw the weapon under a nearby bunk. Peterson helped carry Hochderffer's body to a bed in an adjacent building. Examining the body, Peterson found a small bullet wound on Hochderffer's left side.

The prosecution also called Arthur Cleveland "Cleve" Hochderffer, who had seen his brother's remains in Jerome the day after the shooting and confirmed George Peterson's description of the location where the bullet entered his brother's body. He had arranged for a doctor to examine the body when it was brought to Fresno, California, for burial.

Dr. T. R. Clark then testified about his examination of the deceased's body. The bullet had entered Rock's body, just under the armpit, between the ninth and tenth ribs on the left side of his body. His opinion was that the bullet could not have entered the body without striking Rock's left arm, had that arm been in the normal position (at his side). On cross-examination, defense counsel Ling put on a demonstration to show that if Hochderffer had been holding his pistol with both hands facing Winnie, the fatal shot would have entered the victim's body where Dr. Clark had described.

Ernest Cox was the first defense witness. Obviously nervous, he had the date of the shooting as February 24, instead of the 23rd. As to the events leading up to the shooting, his testimony was essentially the same as the earlier witnesses. He was in the kitchen when Hochderffer entered, heard the exchange of words, saw Rosenberger reach for his rifle and Hochderffer reach up on a shelf, catch the scabbard, and grab the butt of the gun. Stepping out of the room, he heard a shot and reentered. Cox believed he was the first person to come into the room after the shot was fired.

Next was Hank Stuckel, who was also at the ranch that morning. He was standing in the doorway between the kitchen where Rosenberger was standing and the front room where Hochderffer was. He saw Rock reach up on a shelf, put his hand on the scabbard, and pull the gun out with his right hand. Stuckel then stepped out of the room, heard the shot, and reentered. He did not see the shot fired. On cross-examination, Stuckel admitted that he did not see Hochderffer with the gun in his hand. He thought he, and not Cox, was the first person to come back in the room after the shot was fired.

Jerome Undertaker W.P. Scott, who had prepared the body for shipment to California and was a member of the coroner's jury,[14] described Hochderffer's wound. Comparing the blood-stained shirt Rock was wearing that morning, he said the hole in the shirt matched the entry wound. A brief back-and-forth between the defense and the prosecution ensued as to whether the shirt was inside out, which defense counsel Ling described as "right-side before." When the prosecution moved to strike the statement, Judge Sloan said he would leave it to the jury to decide which was the right and left side of the shirt.

Jerome Justice of the Peace W.S. Adams, who had presided over the coroner's inquest, described Hochderffer's wound as being under Rock's left arm. Asked to recount some of the testimony at the inquest, he recalled both Jim Bailey and James Black saying they had seen Hochderffer put his hand on the gun before they left the room.

Jerome Town Marshall Fred Hawkins was also on the coroner's jury and offered similar testimony about the entry wound. Two remaining witnesses, Charles H. Hooker (who had helped post Winnie's bail) and B.H. Scudder, offered similar testimony. The prosecution cross-examination centered on whether the members of the coroner's jury knew each other and that Ernest Cox, one of the ranch owners, was on the Jerome School Board. Perhaps, D.A. Morrison suggested through his questions, Benjamin Scudder's desire to be reappointed to another term as school principal might have influenced his agreement with the inquest findings.

Winnie Rosenberger testified in his own defense. He told of the events leading up to the shooting, how on the morning of the shooting he had asked Rock Hochderffer to leave the ranch. Rock replied,

"I don't know if I will or not." To which Winnie retorted, "You will if I get that gun." Rock then said, "Not if I get mine first." Then both went for their guns. Winnie knew where Rock's gun was, as he had seen it the night before. As he was reaching for his rifle, Winnie looked up and saw Rock facing him with his pistol in both hands pointed directly at Winnie. "I fired as quickly as I could because I was expecting to get shot at any moment." After the shooting, Winnie called for the others and asked them to see what they could do for him. "I told Peterson that I had nothing against him but guessed I had hurt his friend." After it was determined that Hochderffer was dead, Winnie rode to Jerome and turned himself in.

Both sides summed up in front of the jury. Reese Ling opened by emphasizing that Winnie's testimony about Rock having the weapon in both hands pointed at Winnie was consistent with the entry wound under Rock's left arm and inconsistent with Rock having been shot in the back. After all, a physician hired by the Hochderffer family had examined Rock's body and agreed that if Rock's arm had not been raised, the entry wound would have been in his left arm and, Ling pointed out, the only witness to speak of a back wound was Rock's friend George Peterson, who observed the wound only when the body was lying face down.

The prosecution argued that Winnie had provoked a quarrel with Rock with the premeditated intention of killing him, emphasizing that Winnie had said to Ernest Cox: "Watch me, I'll show him this morning." Rosenberger had placed his Winchester in a handy position, as if he was ready for trouble. District Attorney Morrison noted the disparity in distance to retrieve their respective weapons: Rock had twelve feet to reach his weapon, while Winnie had only nine.

Reese Ling's closing argument emphasized that the prosecution had no answer for the location of the fatal wound, telling the jury that he was not asking for sympathy for Winnie Rosenberger, only justice under the law of Arizona, which gives one the right to protect their own life, even to the extent of taking life.

After three days of trial, the jury retired to deliberate at 5:00 p.m. On the first of what would be five ballots, there were eight votes for Not Guilty and four for the lesser offense of Manslaughter. Over the course of subsequent ballots, the four switched to Not Guilty. At 8:00 p.m., the bailiff was told the jury had reached a verdict and was ready to announce it in open court. There was just one problem: Judge Sloan was not available. After he had instructed the jury and left them to deliberate, he had accepted an invitation to go "automobiling" with a friend in one of those "new-fangled motor machines." Their route took them by a local target range where a stray bullet found the vehicle's front tire. A local man, Ralph Tilton, came along in another machine, only to have his own vehicle break down. Not until midnight did Judge Sloan finally arrive back at the courthouse. The parties and their lawyers were called in, and the jury announced its verdict on May 17, 1907: Not Guilty. The jurors were polled individually, each confirming their vote to acquit.

The reaction from the Hochderffer family and their friends was understandably grim. Brother Cleveland "Cleve" Hochderffer was the only family member to attend the trial. Still, the family and their supporters clung to the belief that Rock had been shot in the back when he was unarmed. After the trial, when word spread around Flagstaff that Winnie, known to be an accomplished rider, might appear on horseback in the Fourth of July parade there, several cowboys announced they were "itching to pull a trigger" on the man they believed had gotten away with Rock Hochderffer's murder. Word of this filtered back to the D.K. Ranch, and Winnie did not show up at the parade.[15]

Postscript

Winnie Rosenberger married Mabel Perry (1885–1956) in 1928 and folded quietly into family life. No one in the Perry family ever heard Winnie speak about what happened that day at the Windmill Ranch.

His marriage to Mabel ended in divorce, and he seems to have lived out his later years quietly. In 1942 he registered for the military draft, listing his address as 24th Street and Indian School Road in Phoenix and his occupation as a cattleman. His association with the Hurley family continued as he listed his place of employment as the Hurley Wholesale Meat Company at 15th Avenue and the Salt River. The Perrys have but one remaining photo of H.V. "Winnie" Rosenberger (1880–1954). Taken at the family ranch in Peoria some fourteen years after the trial, but while he and Mabel were still together, the photo shows a serious-looking man in a suit and tie in the back row, standing behind and to Mabel's right. The photo, taken by my grandmother Maud Perry Daly (1887–1973), shows her husband, Frank Daly (1886–1956), holding my mother, Patricia Daly (1918–1999), Winnie's niece, sitting on her father's knee.

Winnie's able defense counsel, Reese M. Ling (1868–1916), did undergraduate work at the Ohio State University and, after coming to Arizona, attended Tempe Normal School (now ASU), graduating in 1886. He received his law degree from the University of Michigan in 1890. He served as Yavapai County Attorney before the trial and Prescott City Attorney afterward. His son David W. Ling (1890–1965), a former county prosecutor and state court judge, was appointed by President Franklin Roosevelt as a U.S. district judge for Arizona in 1936; he served until his death in 1964. Richard Sloan, the judge in Winnie's trial, would go on to serve as the last territorial governor of Arizona. Judge Sloan was instrumental in convincing President Taft to sign the enabling legislation in 1912, despite Taft's reservation about Arizona's proposed constitution. In a perfect world, Sloan should have been Arizona's first post-statehood federal judge. But like Taft, who nominated him, Sloan was a Republican, and Arizona's two Democratic senators, Henry Fountain Ashurst and Mark Smith, blocked his confirmation.

The first Perry Picnic: Perry Ranch circa 1921—photo taken by Maud Perry Daly

THE SEARCH FOR EFFIE DEE

It began innocently enough. The Perry family was having its annual reunion. This time at a park near the territorial capital, Prescott—chosen so that some of the older generation, by this time living in the Arizona Pioneers' Home, could attend.

I had remembered to bring a tape recorder along to gather some impressions about the old days. Amidst screaming kids and barking dogs, I sat down across from Leonard Redden. By then in his eighties, Leonard was a favorite of my grandmother, Maud Perry Daly. He was still lean and trim despite his advancing years. I found him to be what a reporter would call a tough interview. Lots of "yups" and "nopes," the kind of witness trial lawyers dread questioning, giving up only what he wants. Still, he was completely engaging, quick of mind, and a good listener.

It was hard to break the ice. When asked about the early days and if he had any special memories, the response was: "Not much. We just got by." There were several people from his generation, those who matured in the 1920s, whom I wanted to ask him about—my grandmother, her sister Mabel, and Mabel's first husband, a colorful character named Winnie Rosenberger.

It was not part of the plan to ask him about my grandfather, Frank Daly, but Leonard must have known him as they were roughly contemporaries. My grandmother had divorced Frank Daly in the

1930s when divorce carried a certain social stigma, especially for a Chandler, Arizona schoolmarm. In those days, it was a custom following a divorce to go through the family photograph album and tear out any photograph of the former spouse.

Some individual photos escaped, so I had some idea of what he was like—a robust man with sparkling eyes and a full head of graying black hair. Irish like my great-grandmother, Mary Agnes Clark Perry, from Massachusetts like the patriarch of the family, my great-grandfather, William Henry Perry.

Leonard, it turned out, knew Frank Daly quite well, and once he got started, I simply listened. He helped me piece together a few pieces of the puzzle of his life. The first pieces were consistent with what I had heard: Frank Daly was an active, good-looking man, something both he and the people he came in contact with were well aware of. He loved people; loved to be around them, to entertain and be entertained by them.

From what I had been able to gather, I knew he must have been a man of real energy, the kind who lights up a room just by being there. And, like many others in every generation of the family, he loved to drink. (Leonard remembered Frank distilling homemade whiskey in the back of the house on East Coronado Street.) I also knew that there must have been many lonely evenings for my grandmother, just as my own mother would later spend—at home alone, worried, angry, apprehensive about what he might be like when he finally did come through the door.

Excited by finally finding someone in the family who not only knew Frank Daly but was willing to talk about him, I pressed Leonard for details. "Oh yeah, he was handsome, enjoyed a party," and, in Leonard's words, was "damned handy with his fists." Acting as if this was something sort of foreign to me, I asked Leonard to tell me more. "If someone got a little rough with him, he would finish them off." It turned out that Frank Daly was, among other things, a bill collector. (Confirmation of this was later found in a classified in the local newspaper: "COLLECTIONS. We get the money. Southwestern Bureau, 319 Heard Building.")

Given the time, when folks in Phoenix had trouble scraping together the ten-cent fare to ride the streetcars from Brill Street to Indian School Road and over to Glendale, it was not so surprising that Frank Daly was "handy with his fists." Leonard remembered Frank driving him to classes at Phoenix College and telling him about a man who, confronted in a building lobby with a past-due bill, "took a poke" at him. Frank ducked the punch and the man's hand broke through and stuck in a glass showcase.

I was fascinated. It was as if Leonard had somehow pulled out a grainy, black-and-white film of my grandfather. And here he was—good-looking, articulate, quick of wit, word, and fist. By now, Leonard had warmed to the task. I peppered him with questions, and he shot back responses. Now Leonard was like a friendly witness on the stand where a good rapport has been established. The questions come quickly and easily, the responses direct and, to a large extent, predictable.

Then came the unexpected. A pause following a response to a question, and almost out of nowhere Leonard volunteered: "He wrote a column." Taken aback, I asked: "He what?!" "He wrote a column for the newspaper. You know, a gossip column." Leonard was not through: "He wrote it under the name of 'Effie Dee.'"

Sensing the blank look on my face, Leonard added: "You know, his initials were 'F. E. D.' He did not want to use his real name, so he used the name 'Effie Dee.'" If Leonard had described a drunken barroom brawl, the sale of a nonexistent bridge, the seducing of another man's wife, or any number of other things, I would not have been terribly surprised. This was a horse of a different color, and I was determined to find out every detail.

Unfortunately, I didn't get around to finding out for quite awhile. Leonard told me as much as he could remember, so I packed up the tape recorder, and we went our own ways. It took a while to get around to transcribing Leonard's interview. Although I would think about what he told me from time to time, when I finally saw his comment in print, I was even more determined to find the columns of that 1920s gossip, Effie Dee.

It proved to be no easy task. Having no idea where to start, I called a friend at the newspaper and asked him how I could go about finding 1920-era columns. My friend directed me to Earl, a retired city editor, who, it turned out, was doing a series of historical "snapshots" for the one-hundredth anniversary of the paper. I gave him the information Leonard had given me. The column, Leonard was pretty sure, was written for the morning newspaper. He thought the column had been written in 1922 or 1923.

Earl agreed to undertake the search, and I anxiously awaited his results. This was easy, I thought to myself. Turn an expert loose in the archives and presto—the words of my own grandfather right in front of me.

It was not so easy. After two weeks of looking, Earl called me with the bad news. He had read nearly every issue of the *Arizona Republican* during 1922 and 1923. Could Leonard have been wrong? Could the column have been written for *The Phoenix Gazette*, the evening paper? Earl went back to the archives. A week or so went by. More bad news. Nothing in *The Gazette* for those dates either.

I decided to take the direct approach. I went to the library myself. Hours of looking. No luck. I decided to call Leonard. The phone book had a listing for Redden Construction. A builder of schoolhouses in his earlier days, Leonard had apparently kept the name of the company active. No answer. No answer at the home listing in Carefree.

There was one other place I could call. Herb Perry, one of my mother's favorite cousins, would have been a young boy in the 1920s. One of the surviving photographs shows Frank Daly with a tough-appearing boy of eight or ten. In his seventies by the time I reached out to him, Herb, as his son and grandson still do, was farming cotton near Buckeye. I telephoned the farmhouse. His wife

Carmella answered: "If anyone would know about Phoenix in the 1920s, it would be Herb."

Herb called back. I told him what I was looking for. He remembered Frank Daly's office was in the Heard Building on Central Avenue—the same building where the newspaper was published. Aha! All he had to do was walk downstairs and deliver drafts of his column. Herb: "Where have you looked?" I described my trips to the Phoenix Library and started going through their microfilm of old editions of the morning paper. Herb: "Find anything?" The answer was nothing much; certainly, no gossip columns written by "Effie Dee" or "Frank Daly" or anyone like that. Lots of interesting stuff, though. Home runs by Babe Ruth and Rogers Hornsby, Jack Dempsey preparing for his next fight, work stoppages and labor trouble everywhere, and a few local political announcements. Herb got me back on subject: "You may be looking in the wrong year. Try around 1925, '26, or '27."

Back to the library archives. I picked the middle of the three years Herb had suggested, 1926. I figured in those pre-air-conditioning days, it would be better to look in the cooler months, November through March. A man smart enough to convince people to pay their bills in those days would not be foolish enough to stay in Phoenix during the summer. Nothing. I poured for hours through the details of 1926. Still nothing. I poured through 1924. Calvin ("Keep Cool With Coolidge") Coolidge was elected President, George W.P. Hunt to another term as governor of Arizona. Still nothing. I was beginning to think Leonard had imagined Effie Dee. I would try to reach Leonard again. I finally reached Leonard's son-in-law, at Redden Construction. He told me that Leonard had sold his home in Carefree and was now living in a retirement home in Tempe.

The next day I drove out to visit Leonard Redden and his wife at their retirement cottage in Tempe. Leonard would be back in the town where William Henry and Mary Agnes Perry had bought a home at the turn of the century so Leonard's mother could attend Tempe

Normal School (now Arizona State University). Approaching eighty-six, Leonard still looked great. He remembered Frank Daly's still on his back porch. I asked him if he'd tried any. His wife answered for him: "He never did take a drink—always afraid it might kill him."

I told Leonard how hard it had been to track down the elusive Effie Dee. We went back over what he remembered. He was certain it was the morning newspaper and that the column appeared regularly.

With some prompting, Leonard was able to narrow his memories of the Effie Dee columns to the first nine months of 1923. Leonard had his appendix removed in late 1922. He remembered having read the paper every day while recuperating. "Look early in 1923," he told me. I went to the list of months Earl had looked at: January, April, July, and October of that year. He had not had enough time, however, to look at March, April, and May of 1923. Leonard agreed that the best place to start would be the cooler months.

Back to the library. By now, my eyes were crossing. Afraid that I might skip over what I was looking for, I made it a point to read something on every page. Columns by Ring Lardner, various editorial cartoons (an increase in the gasoline tax was just as unpopular in those days), hints to housewives, and a seemingly endless serialized novel by a fellow named Oppenheimer.

And then, on page three of Section Two of the *Arizona Republican* for Friday, March 9, 1923, there it was. "The Valley Tattler." It was written in a distinctive verse-like style, signed at the bottom exactly the way Leonard had said it would be: "Effie Dee."

It was like finding the proverbial needle in a haystack—only this needle not only had a sharp point, but wit and charm. I read and reread every word, which were entirely consistent with the picture of the Frank Daly that Leonard Redden had painted for me. Effie Dee pokes fun at the pompous, winks at Prohibition, and gives more than a fair hint of the kind of life he led. He refers to an attractive woman in town as: "One of the few girls I know of who can be indiscreet discreetly."

Effie Dee describes a man trying to weasel his way out of jury service by telling the judge he is hard of hearing. The judge asks him if he can hear a nickel drop on a counter. A friend on the jury answers for him: "You bet he can, Judge, he could hear a dollar bill drop on a blanket."

In another column, Effie Dee describes a businessman dictating a telegram to be sent to a friend in New Mexico. "Tell him I will meet him on Saturday in Albuquerque." The secretary: "How do you spell Albuquerque?" The businessman: "A smart girl like you doesn't know how to spell it?" The secretary: "You're so smart, you tell me how to spell it." The businessman: "Tell him I'll meet him in Santa Fe."

The past had come to life for me. My middle namesake, the man I knew little of, was a larger part of me than I would have ever imagined or felt possible.

LINE OF DUTY

It was just past midnight, five days into February 1925. Phoenix Police Officer Haze Burch was on night patrol in his Model A Ford. The month before, the city had suffered an unusual rash of burglaries and petty thefts. The conventional wisdom, gathered at the barbershop in the Adams Hotel, was divided as to whether those responsible were local joyriders, "loafing specimens of the home product" as the local newspaper called them, or part of the stream of down-and-out passers-through on their way to California.

Officer Burch pointed his car east on Jefferson past Seventh Street. As he approached Eighth Street, he saw a distinctive red touring car, a Nash with Oklahoma plates. Just up the block stood two men near a parked car on the opposite side of the street. Burch sensed immediately what they were doing: siphoning gasoline. This was not unusual; people passing through without money often tried to fill up their tanks this way as they passed through the desert.

Although alert, Officer Burch had no reason to sense danger. A stern but affable man, he had been constable of the East Phoenix Justice Court for six years and a candidate for Maricopa County Sheriff before joining the police department. He had a reputation of a peacemaker. When he served process on parties, he would often counsel them on the expense and risk of litigation and encourage them to resolve their disputes before they got to court.

Phoenix was a small town then, about thirty thousand robust citizens living in the Sonoran Desert before the days of air-conditioning. Like many peace officers of his day, Officer Burch prided himself on knowing his town, who belonged and who did not, what was out of place and what was not.

Approaching the two young men, Officer Burch left his weapon holstered. A few feet away, he announced his presence. One of the men turned toward him. A kid, Burch thought. He could not be more than eighteen or nineteen. The dark complexion and facial features made Burch think he might even be part Native American. The other man, shorter with lighter hair, did not turn. He had one hand on the hose coming out of the gas tank. Burch could not see his other hand.

"Evening, boys," the tall officer told them. Burch wanted to get their attention but not alarm them. Experience told him not to make more of a situation than was necessary. There might even be a good explanation for what the young men were up to. Perhaps one had run out of gas and was borrowing some from the other.

Burch stopped two or three feet from the young men. Pointing to the other vehicle, Officer Burch asked, "Is this your car?" "No, sir," answered the younger one as he swept a mane of black hair off his forehead and pointed at the red Nash across the street. "Well, boys, I am afraid I am going to have to take you in," Burch told them.

Closing the distance between them, he reached for his handcuffs with his left hand and then snapped one cuff around the wrist of the younger man. As he reached out for the other man, he found himself staring down the barrel of a .44-caliber pistol. "Don't be stupid, son," Officer Burch said to the man as calmly as he could. The voice that responded was not of a frightened kid, but of someone no stranger to these circumstances: "Officer, I'll kill you if you try that."

It was too late. Officer Burch was already reaching to handcuff the second man. The first shot shattered Burch's right hand. A second shot quickly followed to his midsection. Falling to the ground, Burch reached for his service revolver with his left hand and managed to empty it at the fleeing pair. None of his shots found their mark.

Burch leaned up against a palm tree near the curb. Herbert Simpson and Robert Taylor, who lived in the 700 block of East Washington, heard shots and stepped outside. The shots also had awakened Andre Dragich, the manager of a rooming house at 713 East Washington, who ran to the side of the fallen officer. "They got me," Burch told Dragich, pointing to two men running down the street. Dragich made sure the officer was as comfortable as possible and then ran back inside to call the police. Two merchant policemen, Ben Clark and Carl Feurrigiel, were on the scene a few minutes later.

Police Chief George O. Brisbois and Chief of Detectives John J. McGrath came quickly to Burch's side. Piecing together the information from Burch and others, Chief Brisbois remembered a Wanted circular that had come to the department the week before describing two Oklahoma brothers, Babe and Will Lawrence, wanted for the June 1924 murder of Joe P. Morgan, a Ft. Worth, Texas deputy sheriff. The automobile the Lawrence brothers had used to flee that scene was described as a bright-red Nash touring sedan with a distinctively disfigured left front hubcap and Oklahoma plates. In their panic after the confrontation with Officer Burch, the Lawrence brothers tried to start the car and then fled on foot, leaving the Nash behind. (A later search of the car revealed a pair of handcuffs belonging to Deputy Morgan.) There was no doubt: The Lawrence brothers had struck again, and they were somewhere in the Phoenix area.

Officer Burch lived most of that day, long enough to identify his assailants from the Wanted poster. "I'll make it alright," he told County Attorney Arthur T. LaPrade and his deputy, Howard Speakman. He was, of course, not alright. A few minutes after 7:00 that evening, Haze Burch became the first Phoenix police officer to die from wounds received in the line of duty.

News of the event galvanized the community. Offers of rewards came in from Governor George W.P. Hunt and dozens of citizens. Peace officers of every type were organized into groups of two and three, and a massive manhunt ensued. The highways leading in and out of the city were literally sealed off. A telegram arrived from Sheriff J.F. Ledbetter of Muskogee, Oklahoma, telling Arizona officials, in no uncertain terms, what they hoped would happen when the Lawrence brothers were captured:

> Will you deliver Will and Babe Lawrence to Oklahoma and Texas? We are certain to break their necks and we don't mean maybe. If you handle the case there and want details, you may subpoena R.D. Jones, Under-Sheriff; John Barger, Court Bailiff; and H.L. Watts, Deputy Sheriff, all of Muskogee. Our talent and resources are at your command.

Two days later, the Lawrence brothers were captured near the crest of Tempe Butte by Tempe City Marshal Ralph L. McDonald and Cruz Reyes, a local pool hall proprietor deputized on the spot. Reyes had spotted the pair near the block "A" on the south side of the Butte and alerted Marshal McDonald to the brothers' location. Cold and tired from two days on the run and sleeping in the Salt River bottom, the brothers surrendered without incident. A .44-caliber Colt pistol and a Winchester 30-30 rifle were found in their possession, as were Officer Burch's handcuffs. After a later and more intensive search by sheriff's deputies, a second pistol was found secreted in Will Lawrence's trousers.

Chief Deputy Sheriff Tom Marks and a carload of deputies met McDonald, Reyes, and the captured Lawrence brothers at the bottom of Tempe Butte. The brothers were quickly spirited away for three hours of questioning at County Attorney Arthur T. LaPrade's office in the Ellis Building at Second Avenue and Monroe. News of the capture quickly spread. Within a half hour, a large crowd gathered out front. Sensing he might have a problem with mob violence, LaPrade ordered the Lawrence brothers taken out the back door and driven directly to the state penitentiary in Florence.

While the caravan of police cars was transporting the Lawrence brothers to Florence, Reverend H.L. Faulkner was delivering Officer Burch's eulogy at the A.H. McLellan Chapel on North Central Avenue. Haze Burch's fellow Phoenix police officers were the pallbearers; the Boy Scouts served as color-bearers. Late in the afternoon of February 7, 1925, Phoenix Police Officer Haze Burch was laid to rest in the Greenwood Memorial Cemetery in Phoenix.

Haze Burch could have had no idea how violent these young men actually were when he approached them that night. It turned out Babe and Will Lawrence had left a trail of armed robberies, stolen cars, and murders behind them as they crisscrossed the country. In addition to the slaying of Deputy Sheriff Morgan in Texas, they were being sought for the murder of Charles Wilson, a Livingston, Montana police officer occurring three months earlier. Following a series of burglaries, the pair led law enforcement officials from multiple jurisdictions on a Bonnie & Clyde-like chase through the mountains of northern Arkansas and southern Missouri. Brought to the Maricopa County Attorney's office following their Tempe Butte capture, Arthur LaPrade found the Lawrence brothers, especially the older one, bold and unrepentant. "I never met an officer whose hand I would shake," Will told him.

Thirteen days after Officer Burch's confrontation with the Lawrence brothers, more than one thousand people crowded the courtroom of Justice of the Peace Clarence E. Ice for their preliminary hearing. LaPrade created a stir by walking into the courtroom with the Lawrence brothers' assorted weaponry: a pair of .44-caliber Colt long-barrel, single-action revolvers and a 30-30 Winchester carbine and two ammunition belts containing dum-dum bullets. After a four-hour hearing, Judge Ice bound the Lawrence brothers over for trial. They were held without bail over vigorous objections of their flamboyant attorney, A.M. de Graffenried, who had traveled from Muskogee, Oklahoma, to represent the brothers. Judge Ice based the bail denial on the serious nature of the crime and evidence that, while in custody in Florence, the brothers had actively planned an escape. William A. "Will" Lawrence and his younger brother Albert Beauregard "Babe" Lawrence were to stand trial for the murder of Officer Burch.

Attorney de Graffenried did not show up for further proceedings. Phoenix lawyer L.C. "Mac" McNabb, however, stepped in and provided the brothers an aggressive defense. Before a trial date could even be set, he asked that the case be removed to federal court where a fairer trial might be obtained. Finding no basis for removal, Superior Court Judge Myron T. Phelps denied the motion. He did, however, grant McNabb's motion to try the brothers separately. This would lead, ultimately, to a decision by County Attorney LaPrade to cooperate with Texas authorities to return Babe Lawrence to face charges in connection with the murder of Deputy Sheriff Morgan. Judge Phelps set a March 24 trial date for Will Lawrence.

This was an especially busy time of year at the Perry farm at 35th Avenue and Lower Buckeye Road. The cotton crop would be planted soon, and the dairy herd needed constant attention. It was dawn to dusk work. Hard stuff, but common for that day. Bill Perry heard a car approach the farmhouse. As it got closer, he recognized it as a sheriff's vehicle. His momentary apprehension, as he wondered whether one of the farmhands had done something wrong, was quickly put to rest. He recognized the deputy sheriff. "I've a jury summons for your dad, Bill," said the deputy. Forty-two-year-old William Kittredge Perry explained that his father, William Henry, was not around at the time. The deputy left the summons with the son. Bill gave the summons to his father at dinner that night. Now in his eighties, the old man had little time for such things. "Take this down and tell 'em I cannot serve. I'm too old, too busy," William Henry told his son.

When the trial of Will Lawrence began as scheduled, the courtroom was again packed. Judge Phelps had made sure there was an extra number of potential jurors. Haze Burch was well known, and the sense of outrage at his killing was widespread. The judge knew it would be difficult to find jurors who either did not know Officer Burch or had not heard of his death. The courtroom clerk began to call the names. When the name William Perry was announced, young Bill Perry stood up.

"Judge, my name is William K. Perry. The summons was sent to my father, William H. Perry, but he is too old and too busy to serve."

Standing, clutching his cowboy hat, Bill Perry waited for the judge to excoriate him or demand that his father show up. The judge's response was not unexpected to seasoned courtroom observers of the day, but it stunned the younger Perry: "You look like a perfectly fine juror yourself, Mr. Perry."

So, the younger Perry was in the jury pool. The defense subjected the panel to extensive questioning, but Bill Perry survived the challenge. He had not known Officer Burch personally and, although he had heard that a police officer had been killed, he knew little of the events and even less about the defendant.

Mac McNabb had his work cut out for him. Capital cases are difficult enough, but where the victim is a police officer it is next to impossible. This was even more true in Arizona in the 1920s. The shooting of Officer Burch, the massive search for his killers, and the apprehension of the Lawrence brothers were front-page banner headlines. There is a cruel irony about the trials of accused police killers. Joseph Wambaugh's chilling novel *The Onion Field* does an excellent job of describing it. Often the defense turns on the victim. The police officer becomes the bad guy. If this is difficult to explain in the abstract, it is even more difficult to explain to a jury, especially twelve men from a small desert community that just one month before had suffered the first line-of-duty death of one of its peacekeepers.

But that was exactly the nature of Will Lawrence's defense. The argument was that the Lawrence brothers were engaged, at the most, in a simple misdemeanor; that Officer Burch had used such excessive force in arresting the brothers that Will Lawrence was justified in doing what he so plainly did.

The defense said they would offer up the testimony of individuals from the community that Officer Burch was a "person of overbearing and aggressive character." Judge Phelps was skeptical. Since the brothers could not have known Burch, how could the officer's state of mind possibly justify Will Lawrence's actions? The defense offered up a witness, a local character named Burt Ogburn, who would testify that Burch had a reputation in the community as "quick on the shoot." Judge Phelps's skepticism remained intact. The jury was excused for one hour while he heard argument on whether to allow the evidence. He would allow the testimony but would limit questions to those calling for a Yes or No response. On cross-examination, County Attorney LaPrade brought out that neither Ogburn nor the several other proposed witnesses knew Officer Burch well. Two of them, it turned out, did not know him at all.

The trial lasted three days. Andre Dragich, the rooming house operator who was quickly at Burch's side after the shooting, testified how Officer Burch had pointed to two men running from the scene, the pair's attempt to start the Nash, and their subsequent flight on foot. Chief Brisbois was allowed to testify about Burch's deathbed identification of the Lawrence brothers, and Will Lawrence in particular, from the Oklahoma Wanted flyer.

To establish the circumstances of Officer Burch's confrontation with the Lawrence brothers, including the history of the unique red Nash, which had been stolen in Oklahoma, the prosecution produced John Barger, a veteran Oklahoma highway patrolman. Barger and Deputy Morgan had arrested the Lawrence brothers in June 1924 on the outskirts of Muskogee, Oklahoma, for the theft of a government-owned Buick. Like Officer Burch, they had assumed the brothers to be less dangerous than they really were. On the ride back to the sheriff's office, Will Lawrence somehow grabbed Morgan's pistol. A struggle ensued and Morgan was fatally shot. Barger was overcome in the melee and then shackled with his own handcuffs. Will and Babe Lawrence then drove down a deserted farm road, dumped Morgan's body, and tied Barger to a tree. "I am here only by the Grace of God," Barger told the Arizona jury.

The trial also produced other emotional moments. To gain admission of Haze Burch's deathbed identification of the Lawrence brothers as his assailants, County Attorney LaPrade had to prove that Burch actually feared death at the moment he made it. Chief of Police Brisbois testified as to Burch's last few words:

> They got me pretty bad. I am a goner. Take care of my wife and babies. I don't think I will make it.

But perhaps the most devastating prosecution witness was Dora Burch, Haze's widow. She was at her husband's side soon after he reached the hospital. "They shot me, Dora, I'm bleeding inside." Before he passed into unconsciousness, Burch told her of finding two men siphoning gas from a car and how the older of the pair had shot him when he attempted to put handcuffs on him.

Mac McNabb elected to put both of the Lawrence brothers on the stand, to bolster their theory that Burch, not the brothers, had been the aggressor. While necessary to portray the scene, the decision produced a cross-examination in which County Attorney LaPrade was able to have Babe Lawrence describe how his brother Will fired shots at Officer Burch. During the prosecution's case, the jury had heard a stenographer recite the content of Will's statement in the county attorney's office following the brothers' Tempe Butte capture, but they would have very likely never have had heard Babe Lawrence identify his own brother as the trigger man had McNabb not put him on the stand.

Chief Deputy County Attorney Howard Speakman delivered the final argument for the State. He seized upon the trail of bloodshed and violence that had preceded the Lawrence brothers coming to Phoenix.

> These were not mere amateurs, trapped in events beyond their control. They are no strangers to police officers doing their duty. They are no strangers to death.

Judge Phelps then instructed the jury. He refused to give a defense-requested instruction that implied the shooting of Officer Burch was justified. The instructions were completed, and the case submitted to the jury at 1:55 p.m. The bailiff took the jurors to lunch, after which they returned to begin deliberations.

Those deliberations did not last long. They retired to deliberate at 2:40 p.m., and just after 3:00 p.m. they sent a note to Judge Phelps. They had reached a verdict. The parties and their lawyers were rounded up and brought to the courtroom. Dora Burch, Haze's widow, was there, as she had been throughout the trial. Will Lawrence sat emotionless, as he had throughout the trial, at the defense table with his mother, Lucy Lawrence, at his side.

There are few moments in life more steeled with emotion than when a jury returns in a criminal trial, even more so in a capital case. Conventional wisdom has it that if jurors will not look at the defendant when they enter the courtroom, he is in big trouble. Will Lawrence and Mac McNabb looked at the jurors; they did not look back.

Judge Phelps took the bench. "Members of the jury, have you reached a decision? "We have, Your Honor." The jury foreman read the verdict:

> We, the members of the jury, duly impaneled, and on our oath, find the defendant William A. Lawrence guilty of murder in the first degree and fix the penalty at death.

Judge Phelps thanked members of the jury and then discharged them. He took a few moments to compliment both the prosecution and the defense. He had particularly kind words for Mac McNabb, the defense attorney. As I reflect on some of the cases I have tried involving people reasonably unpopular at the time, it is difficult to imagine the burden McNabb must have been under. Even the local newspaper, which would have gladly seen the trial suspended with a quick lynching to follow, had to compliment McNabb on the eloquence of his spoken word and the resoluteness of his efforts to defend Will Lawrence. Later in April, Judge Phelps listened to and denied various post-trial motions filed by the defense.

Lawrence's appeal was heard by the Supreme Court of Arizona in October 1925.[16] Mac McNabb argued for Will, Attorney General John W. Murphy for the State. A central issue was the way in which the jury panel had been drawn. According to the law of the day, jurors were to come from a list of qualified voters supplied by the County Board of Supervisors. The list from which the Lawrence jury was picked contained six thousand names, while there were some 17,000 registered voters in the county. Only by implication of this math did the defense make any note of the lack of women in the jury pool. Arizona voters, after all, had approved the right of women to vote in 1914—six years before the ratification of the 19th Amendment. The Supreme Court Opinion, written by Justice Alfred C. Lockwood, determined this shortfall did not affect the ultimate result. There is no mention in the opinion that the William Perry who served on the jury was not the one actually called to duty, but his son.[17]

The Supreme Court of Arizona affirmed Will Lawrence's conviction and death penalty on November 6, 1925. The Supreme Court of the United States denied Lawrence's certiorari petition one month later. There is no record of any attempt at post-judgment writs.

Eleven months after the Jefferson Street confrontation, Will Lawrence turned twenty-seven in his cell on condemned row in the Arizona State Prison in Florence, awaiting his march to the gallows.

The night before facing the hangman's noose, he spent time with his mother and his sixteen-year-old sister, Fay Jean Lawrence, a Phoenix high school girl. Mac McNabb was also there. One of Will's last wishes was to speak with his brother Babe, by then serving a life sentence in Texas for the slaying of Deputy Morgan. The request was refused. He received the expected news that the governor would not commute his sentence. Prison Warden R.B. Sims made sure that the hangman's noose was visible through the window in his cell door.

Lawrence asked for a guitar shortly before his 5:00 a.m. scheduled execution. There was a stillness and silence throughout the prison. Will sang from a popular hymn of the day:

> Somewhere, somewhere,
> Beautiful Isle of Somewhere;
> Land of the true where we live anew,
> Beautiful Isle of Somewhere

Warden Sims was impressed by Will's courage. He had seen eleven men executed during his tenure, watching their bravado turn to varying stages of fear as the moment of truth approached. This man displayed little of that.

The guards arrived and fastened Will's arms behind him. "I'd like to sing you another song, Mac, but it looks like we don't have time," he told his attorney. There were about twenty or so people present, including the first woman allowed to view an Arizona execution. One month short of a year from his confrontation with Officer Burch and unrepentant to the end, Will Lawrence paid the ultimate price.

Postscript

Officer Burch left behind two sons and an infant daughter. One of those sons, Frank Haze Burch, five years old at the time, would become a prominent member of the Arizona legal community. A founding partner of the Burch & Cracchiolo firm, he is a member of the Maricopa County Bar Association Hall of Fame and a founder of the ASU Law Society (giving its charter class—including Joe Sims, the late Mike Gallagher, and me—an instant alumni association). Frank Haze Burch was honored in 1990 by the American Jewish Committee with its Humanitarian Award. At the age of thirty, as a member of the Phoenix Union School Board, four years prior to *Brown v. Board of Education*, Haze had moved to end the segregation of the races in its public schools. He was always quite modest about this. "It was just the right thing to do," he always said.

And, oh yes, that elderly farmer who sent his son to explain his absence to Judge Phelps? That was William Henry Perry (1844–1929), a pioneer Arizona farmer and my great-grandfather. The son who served in his place, William Kittredge Perry (1883–1954), was my great-uncle, the older brother of my grandmother, Maud Perry Daly (1887–1973). His grandson and great-grandson, also named William Perry, carry on the family farming tradition west of Buckeye, Arizona.

PERRY CHILDREN

Henry Jones Perry (1874–1948)—The eldest and only sibling not born in Arizona, he was known as "Jones" and raised cattle and engaged in mining. He passed away at Bracker's Rest Home in Tempe. Cremation was at the Greenwood Memorial Park in Phoenix and his ashes were scattered near Badger Springs.

Charlotte Elizabeth Perry (1876–1958)—The oldest daughter, she was born at Johnny Osborne Springs, Arizona Territory, during one of the sheep drives to the San Francisco Peaks area. She was married for thirty-six years to Homer Redden, who did the pen-and-ink drawing of the Perry Ranch on the Agua Fria River. "Lottie," as she was known, is buried in Double Butte Cemetery in Tempe.

Mary Adeline Perry (1878–1903)—Born at the family home at Badger Springs, she married Joseph Reuben Bassett in 1902 in Phoenix, witnessed by her brother William Kittredge Perry and sister Grace. She died giving birth to Walter Bassett (father of Perry Bassett and Sharon Farr) on February 4, 1903, in Safford, Arizona Territory. She is buried in the Masonic Pioneer Cemetery in Phoenix.

Grace Perry (1881–1963)—Born at the family home at Badger Springs, she married Carl Harvey of Vermont in 1908 in Tempe in a ceremony witnessed by brother William Kittredge and sister Maud.

Passed away in 1963 at the age of eighty-one. She is buried in Hillcrest Memorial Park in Bakersfield, California.

William Kittredge Perry (1883–1954)—Also born at Badger Springs, he was a cattleman and later a dairy farmer in Peoria. Like Jones Perry, he was involved in mining and filed location claims for mines, including one for the Relief Gold Mine in the Maricopa Mining District, joined with his brother-in-law Francis E. Daly (husband of his younger sister Maud). He married Theresa Nellie (Nell) Whelan in 1916 in Phoenix. They had two sons: Paul (father of Lisa Perry, Gina Ragsdale, and Dugie Heiden) and William Herbert (father of Bill Perry, Anna Marie Perry, Paul Perry, Tom Perry, and Gigi Aja). William Kittredge died in 1954 at the age of seventy in Peoria. Cremation was in the Greenwood Memorial Park in Phoenix.

Mabel Perry (1885–1956)—Born at Badger Springs, she married Henry Vincent Rosenberger in 1907 in Tempe, Arizona Territory, in a ceremony witnessed by her sisters Grace and Maud. That marriage ended in divorce in 1921. Mabel was briefly married to Deo Clair "Doc" Allen and later married Arthur Haynes in 1930, a marriage that lasted until Arthur's death in 1954. She lived for years across the street from the Westward Ho Hotel. Mabel died in 1956 in Phoenix. Burial was in the Double Buttes Cemetery in Tempe.

Maud Perry (1887–1973)—Born at the Badger Springs family ranch, she attended Phoenix Union High School and then Tempe Normal School (now ASU) and later earned a master's degree from Arizona State College (now NAU) in Flagstaff. She and Francis E. Daly were married in Bisbee, Arizona, in 1917, a marriage that ended in divorce in 1931. They had two children, Patricia Agnes (mother of Barry, Michael, and Mary Hawkins) and Frances Elaine (mother of Edward, Maeve, and Henry Perry). She died at the age of eighty-one in a nursing home in Cottonwood. Burial was in the Double Buttes Cemetery in Tempe.

Agnes Perry (1890–1924)—The youngest Perry girl, Agnes was born at the family ranch near Cordes, Arizona Territory. She attended Tempe Normal School and followed her sister Maud as the editor of the *Tempe Daily News* (now *The State Press*). In 1920, Agnes married Thanks Anderson in 1920. He served as an artillery officer with the U.S. Army in France during World War I. He carried a picture of her with him during his wartime service. Agnes passed away from complications of scarlet fever. Burial was at the Double Buttes Cemetery in Tempe.

Eben Prescott Perry (1892–1962)—The youngest of the Perry siblings. Born at the family ranch, he enlisted in the U.S. Marine Corps on September 28, 1917, in Phoenix and served in the Philippines and China. He was discharged on December 4, 1919. On Christmas Day, 1922, he married Ottilia (Tilly) Luke, whose brother Frank Luke, Jr. was a World War I fighter pilot and Medal of Honor recipient. Luke Air Force Base is named for him. Eben and Tilly were unable to have children of their own but took in scores of foster children and adopted three (Frank Luke Smith, Gerald Prescott, and Mary Louise). Eben died in Prescott and is buried in the Fort Whipple Veterans Memorial Cemetery there.

WINSLOW INTRODUCTION

The stories that follow spring out of growing up in Winslow, Arizona, an experience Phyllis and I shared. We were in the same schools from junior high to high school. We went on to college together, got married during our junior year, and have been together since. Her father, Leo Lewis, was one of the town doctors. "The Flournoy Fireplug" is her father's story and recounts how Phyllis and her family came to call Winslow home.

My father, Bert Hawkins, came to Arizona from East Texas in the teeth of the Great Depression for a job with President Roosevelt's Civilian Conservation Corps (CCC). He worked in a camp that built hiking trails and fish hatcheries, making $30 a month, $20 of which was sent home. When his time with the CCC came to an end, he signed on with Standard Oil, training to be a gas station operator. The training station was in Phoenix at the corner of Central Avenue and Van Buren. One day, Patty Daly, a young girl from Chandler, drove in for a fill-up. He won her over with a bright smile. They soon married, had my brother Barry at Good Samaritan Hospital, and headed to Winslow to operate a station there.

The sun setting behind the San Francisco Peaks,
so deeply blue against the orange and red of the
cloud blankets.

The eastbound freight that used to steam out of
Winslow and whistle to top speed at the
stockyards, just as I was falling asleep every
night on the back porch.

The view of the Painted Desert and the
thoughts of the Indians who lived so
beautifully behind those buttes, far behind
and away up to Utah and way over from
Grand Canyon east to the red cliff country
around Gallup. Sheep and good horses, and dances
and songs and jewelry and mystery
and inhabited mountains.

"Memories of Winslow" September 1, 1942
Journals of Wm. P. Mahoney, Jr.

THE WINSLOW BOYS

They remain the legends of my hometown. People who excelled not simply on the platform of the railroad town our families shared, but on the larger stage of life. They knew governors, senators, and presidents, who in turn respected their counsel. They represented potential achieved, status accomplished and hopes honored. They knew great success and endured bitter failure. In background and philosophy, they could not have been more different: one the Irish Catholic son of a labor organizer who wore the label "liberal" proudly, and the other an Episcopalian son from middle-class German stock who was conservative before being conservative was cool. At the pinnacle of their careers, they worked for John F. Kennedy and Richard M. Nixon, two presidents whose lives dominated many of the great issues of the last half of the twentieth century. Both knew the aura of success at the highest levels of power, and both saw how quickly success can turn to tragedy.

They were William P. Mahoney, Winslow High School Class of 1934, and Richard G. Kleindienst, Winslow High School Class of 1941. For the impressionable youth of our tight-knit community that followed along after them, they were the gold standard of achievement, the makers of the mark. Within three months of each other in 1999, they were gone, and for my own memories of the small-town experience we shared, things will not seem the same without them.

We all had the same high school government teacher, Miss Verla Oare. For forty years, Miss Oare taught American government to every student who passed through the doors of Winslow High School. My own turn came in 1962, more than twenty years after Richard Kleindienst and almost thirty years after Bill Mahoney. Richard Kleindienst was by then a prominent Phoenix attorney and Republican Party activist, involved in Barry Goldwater's planned presidential bid and preparing his own run for governor of Arizona, but several years away from service in the Nixon Administration. Bill Mahoney was serving the Kennedy Administration as United States ambassador to Ghana. Although I would later come to both know and admire him, his family had left Winslow in the late 1930s, so at this point Bill Mahoney was simply a name to me.

Richard Kleindienst was another matter. The family, as it had been for several generations, was an active part of town life. Richard's grandfather, Joseph Kleindienst, a short and feisty man of German descent, had arrived in Winslow in 1909, three full years before Arizona became a state. In a railroad town of some 1,800 souls—1,780 of whom were probably card-carrying union members and Democrats—Joe Kleindienst was a staunch and unrepentant Republican. His party ties earned him a treasured salaried job during the 1920s and early 1930s: local postmaster during the Harding, Coolidge, and Hoover administrations.

Granddad, as Richard called him, thought Franklin Delano Roosevelt was the personification of all he found reprehensible about Democrats. Joe was quite influential in young Richard's development, dragging him out one early October morning in 1936 to meet Governor Alfred M. Landon of Kansas, the Republican nominee for President. "Alf," as he was popularly known, was on his way to campaign in California, and when his train stopped briefly in Winslow, Grandpa Joe pushed young Richard to the front of the line for an autograph and a pat on the head.

The election of November 1936 saw Alf Landon crushed by President Roosevelt. That election result produced an event that had a searing effect on Richard Kleindienst. Giddy with joy over Roosevelt's landslide election and full of piss and vinegar (as my father would say) from a night of drinking (then and now Winslow's primary form of indoor entertainment), a group of locals appeared in the front yard of the Kleindienst home (Richard's father Al and grandfather Joe lived next door to each other) shouting, "Get out of Arizona, Joe Kleindienst. Get out of the United States. You're not an American."[18] Never one to back away from a fight, old Joe came out on the porch with a .45 revolver in his hand and challenged the crowd. "Any son-of-a-bitch who thinks he is big enough to run me and my family out of this town, come on up and try!" No one took up the challenge, and the crowd disbursed. Thirteen-year-old Richard was frightened to tears by these events, but his granddad put a comforting arm around him, saying, "Don't worry, Dickie. In politics, there is always another day."

At about the same time as Richard Kleindienst was being frightened by the election-night mob in Winslow, Bill Mahoney was a student at the University of Notre Dame. A veritable Renaissance man, Bill Mahoney's Winslow career was the stuff of legends. Like Richard Kleindienst would be several years later, Bill was student body president and an honor student. A gifted athlete who set state and national records in the hurdles, Bill was also a star halfback on the football team. His musical abilities—on the clarinet and with his voice—won music competitions at what is now Northern Arizona University. His writing talents earned him a job as a stringer for *The Prescott Courier*, the newspaper with the largest circulation in northern Arizona in those days. He would write about the goings on of the day—a Hollywood celebrity aboard the Santa Fe Super Chief, Cardinal Pacelli (later Pope Pius XII) stopping briefly at the airport—and then put the result on the westbound train for publication in the next afternoon's paper.[19] He also saw the effects of the Great Depression firsthand:

> Literally hundreds of families were smugly called "Okies" and "Arkies" passed through Winslow on U.S. 66 during any week fleeing from the terrible drought and windstorms that had destroyed their farms. It was not unusual to see a family of five or six—father, mother and children—crowded in an old Model T Ford, flat broke, trying to reach the promised land of California. Comparable hundreds of "bums" rode the rails on every freight train passing through—even behind the engine on passenger trains.[20]

Mahoney's track talents earned him a scholarship to Notre Dame, a larger stage where he continued to excel. These were heady days at Notre Dame; the legendary Knute Rockne had coached the Fighting Irish football team to six national championships from 1919 to 1930. The track coach, John Patrick Nicholson, would later gain fame as the coach of the British team whose story was told in the movie *Chariots of Fire*. Notre Dame's track squad regularly competed against Ohio State, and Bill Mahoney, the lanky nineteen-year-old from Winslow, found himself competing against none other than OSU's Jesse Owens. In one memorable contest in 1935, Owens edged Mahoney at the wire, both men breaking the existing world record for the event. Afterward, Bill sought out the man whose Olympic accomplishments would burn a hole in Hitler's racism, only to be told by some of Owens's Ohio State teammates, "He's not here—he's staying down with the n____ers."[21] If the drunken mob on his grandfather's lawn was Richard Kleindienst's defining moment of political maturity, the sheer hypocrisy of this moment was Bill Mahoney's.

Richard Kleindienst caught the eye of Miss Verla Oare the moment he entered Winslow High School. He was a star debater, helping

Miss Oare's team win the regional debate tournament for four years running. In the spring of 1940, relying on a coalition of what he described as minorities and "non-jocks," Richard Kleindienst was elected student body president of Winslow High, defeating football captain Jimmy Upchurch by one vote. Richard had lost his mother in 1937, and in Verla Oare he found a surrogate. She told him how to dress and how to comport himself, and she even pleaded with the school superintendent to re-admit him following an incident in which the student body president was caught with a jar of liquor at a school dance.

During at least one of his summer vacations, Richard Kleindienst worked in my father's Texaco station. A New Deal Democrat from Texas, Dad had experienced the Depression firsthand and attributed his survival to FDR's Civilian Conservation Corps. He nonetheless had great respect for Al Kleindienst's son. Richard was an energetic worker and "good with the customers." Following graduation from high school, Richard attended the University of Arizona briefly and then, following a two-and-a-half-year stint in the Air Force, was admitted to Harvard. Verla Oare played a large part in securing his admission and Richard did not disappoint her, graduating with undergraduate honors and then magna cum laude from Harvard Law School. While in law school, a friend at the Harvard Business School introduced Richard to Margaret Elizabeth Dunbar. Within six weeks, they were engaged and then married. It was a cheery event in a bleak year for Richard, as he watched the Republicans snatch defeat from the jaws of victory in the 1948 Truman-Dewey race.

Richard was in Winslow during a Christmas holiday that I will never forget. My brother Barry's present that year was a pellet pistol, the kind that pumps up. Mom was dead set against it; she didn't mutter, "You'll shoot your eye out" like Melinda Dillon in *A Christmas Story*, but it was the same sentiment. A day or two after Barry got his pistol, a neighbor's son came home with a pellet lodged in his heel, claiming that my brother had shot him. Dad called Richard, who dropped what he was doing and came to the house. After a couple of drinks and a demonstration of the pellet pistol's inability to penetrate shoe leather, Richard concluded that the incident simply could not have occurred in the way the boy was claiming. Richard paid a visit to the family and calmly convinced them to question their son more carefully. This resulted in an admission that the shooting had actually involved an accident with another neighborhood boy's .22 rifle and that my brother was not involved at all. Richard's effort saved my brother a lifetime of explaining and left a lasting impression on me.

While Richard Kleindienst's military service was brief and uneventful—it occupies all of one line in his memoirs—Bill Mahoney's was anything but. Graduating magna cum laude in 1939 and completing law school at Notre Dame in two years, he obtained a commission in the U.S. Navy (after, in a three-week flurry, passing the Indiana, Illinois, and Arizona bar examinations). He spent a brief tour in California, where he linked up with a group of other naval officers at Mare Island, some of them former college and pro football players, and put together a team that regularly beat up on the Pac-10 squads of the day. Travel with the team permitted him some free time, and on one trip, he met Alice Phelan Doyle in Carmel. He was on the brink of receiving orders for service in the Pacific, but it was clear he had found the love of his life.

With mixed emotions, Bill Mahoney steamed out of San Francisco in December 1944. After a brief stay in Hawaii, he found himself on Wake Island and several of the atolls in the area, including Kwajalein and Roi Namur. Assigned to a Combat Air Services unit, Bill acted as a jack-of-all-trades, coordinating athletic events, counseling sailors and airmen with disciplinary problems, and even serving as a stand-in chaplain when the only Roman Catholic priest in the area rotated stateside. "They must have figured that anyone from Notre Dame could substitute," Bill recalled.

August 1945 saw the bombing of Hiroshima and Nagasaki and the end of the war in the Pacific, but Bill Mahoney would be deeply involved in its aftermath. As American forces freed American and British prisoners of war on many of the reclaimed Pacific islands, they were faced with repeated descriptions of atrocities committed by Japanese forces. Although not as well known as the Nuremberg trials, the Japanese War Crime Trials produced a number of dramatic and sad stories.[22] Bill Mahoney led the prosecution team in two of them: the trial of Admiral Sakaibara, the notorious commander of the Wake Island garrison; and the subsequent trial of Admiral Abe, accused of responsibility for the beheading of nine American Marine POWs who had been captured on Makin Atoll. Both Sakaibara and Abe were found guilty and hanged.[23]

The years following World War II found the Winslow Boys back in Arizona and immersed in politics. Bill Mahoney went to work for Arizona Attorney General John Sullivan and found himself working in the same building where his father had served in the Arizona Legislature (1915–1918). The Mahoney roots were as deeply Democratic as the Kleindienst's were Republican. A former labor organizer—he once headed the Snowball Miners' Union—William Patrick Mahoney, Sr. had ventured down from Butte, Montana, to Oatman, Arizona Territory, in 1902. He married into the Fitzgerald family, whose patriarch had arrived in Prescott in 1871.[24] Following his legislative service, Bill's father was elected to four successive terms as sheriff of Mohave County (1918–1924). When the voters "retired" him in 1924, Mahoney, Sr. took a job as chief special agent of the Albuquerque Division of the Santa Fe Railroad. The division ran from Albuquerque, New Mexico, to Needles, California, and its headquarters was in Winslow.

By the early 1950s, the Winslow Boys were headed down essentially the same path, albeit on different sides of the street. Bill Mahoney became active in the Arizona Democratic Party and was elected in 1952 as Maricopa County Attorney. That same year began to produce the "other day" that Richard Kleindienst's grandpa had promised on the porch in Winslow sixteen years earlier: Richard was elected to the Arizona House of Representatives. He had gone door-to-door in a district that had elected Democrats for years. Miss Oare's prized debate student was all of twenty-nine years old and the youngest member of the Arizona Legislature. The influx of World War II veterans had begun to change Arizona's political landscape, and the landslide election of General Eisenhower to the presidency provided powerful coattails, helping elect a number of Republicans. One of them was Phoenix City Councilman Barry Goldwater, who upset Ernest "Mac" MacFarland, the sitting majority leader of the United States Senate.

Bill Mahoney's entry into elective politics proved one of the few Democratic success stories of 1952. One of only three Maricopa County Democrats who survived the Republican sweep, he threw himself into his county attorney duties with passion and energy. He soon found that too much of either can be a bad mix for a public prosecutor. In his first prosecution, he sought a murder conviction of a retired police detective who had shot his daughter after she was diagnosed with incurable cancer. Bill saw it as a case of straightforward first-degree murder and, with the assistance of one of the bright stars of the office—Thomas Tang[25]—presented the case as such. The jury, aided by a powerful argument of Dow Ben Roush, saw it differently; deliberating less than a half hour, they acquitted.

The local press, principally *The Arizona Republic*, was critical at every step of the new county attorney's tenure. For his part, Bill did not shy away from controversy when he thought the cause was right—such as the effort to desegregate Arizona's public schools.[26] Early in his term when he made what he thought was an entirely routine announcement—that his office would enforce a court decision that Arizona's anti-gambling laws forbade bingo games—the headlines blared "Mahoney to Close Bingo."[27]

The year 1954 saw the Democrats make something of a come-back. The demands of his law practice forced Richard Kleindienst to forego seeking reelection to the Arizona House. Nationally, the Republicans lost the control of Congress that they had gained only two years earlier. In Arizona, Republicans lost the governor's chair and most of their legislative gains. Congressman John Rhodes managed to survive, but, as Richard Kleindienst described it, "only by an eyewink."[28] Meanwhile, despite the efforts of the press to defeat him, Bill Mahoney was reelected as Maricopa County Attorney.

The year 1956 proved eventful for the Winslow Boys. Richard Kleindienst, with Barry Goldwater's active support, was elected chairman of the Arizona Republican Party. Bill Mahoney, meanwhile, decided to go after the congressional seat of John Rhodes. He looked to have a good chance—Democrats enjoyed a considerable edge in voter registration and, despite his sometimes-spotty press, his service as county prosecutor had given him excellent name recognition across much of the district.

Bill Mahoney made one serious tactical mistake: He came out against Arizona's "Right to Work" law, a measure that effectively meant that workers who organized a union could not speak for non-members in the bargaining process. The issue became quite popular among the many World War II returning veterans, who had no particular allegiance to unions and saw any requirement of union membership as a bar to full employment. Bill Mahoney saw the issue through the eyes of the many union members who had helped his father's political career and then his own; to them, it was an anti-union measure, pure and simple. Against the advice of a number of his supporters, Mahoney came out against "Right to Work." On election day, the front page of *The Arizona Republic* contained a black-bordered editorial written by publisher Eugene Pulliam saying: "Remember when you go to the polls today that Bill Mahoney is Walter Reuther's Stooge."[29] Reuther was the head of the United Auto Workers; in Arizona, this was somewhat like saying you were a friend of Joe Stalin. Bill Mahoney lost the race by a thousand votes, or less than one-half of one percent of the total votes cast. He was certainly not done with politics, but he would never seek elective office again.

The 1960s saw the Winslow Boys turn their attention to national politics. Bill Mahoney and a group of allies[30] pulled off a minor miracle by delivering the Arizona delegation to the 1960 Democratic National Convention, not to Lyndon Baines Johnson as Arizona's senior senator, Carl Hayden, had wished, but to another senator, John F. Kennedy. The vote was agonizingly close (403–401), but the party followed the "Unit Rule" in those days and the entire delegation had to cast its convention votes in the way the majority demanded. In the course of the ensuing campaign, Bill Mahoney met Ted and Robert Kennedy and had several phone conversations with their older brother, the future President.

Richard Kleindienst's own political activity only increased in the aftermath of Richard Nixon's narrow loss in 1960 to John F. Kennedy. Already a trusted advisor of the senator's, Kleindienst became part of the team that would eventually secure the 1964 Republican nomination for Barry Goldwater. A man of undeniable energy, Richard Kleindienst may have, to borrow another of my father's expressions, "bitten off more than he could chew" during this period. In addition to the demands of his law practice and despite his duties as Senator Goldwater's delegate coordinator, he took on the task of running for governor of Arizona. He won his primary, defeating a then-little-known car dealer and state senator named Evan Mecham, but he lost the general election to Sam Goddard.[31]

The post-war careers of both Mahoney and Kleindienst were framed, in large part, by early alliances in the world of politics. Politics is a strange business. You find your star attached to the comet-like force of a particular personality. That force can pull you to great heights, but when it crashes, so do you. Both Winslow Boys would feel the thrill of the ride up and the hard fall that followed.

Bill Mahoney found himself attached to the Kennedys and, in the early 1960s, no constellation of stars was rising faster or looked like it would last longer. It was an easy liaison for Mahoney; he had an instant affection for JFK and a deep attachment to Robert Kennedy.

President Kennedy did not forget the Arizonans who had turned the state delegation away from Lyndon Johnson. In February 1962, the President called and asked Bill Mahoney if he would consider becoming an ambassador. After some soul-searching, Bill agreed, closed down his law practice, and headed for Washington. He soon found himself posted to the African nation of Ghana, which was in the midst of the post-colonial struggle between the West and the forces of the Soviet Union.[32]

Bill Mahoney was in the Oval Office on November 19, 1963, on his way back to Africa. He and President Kennedy talked about the events of the day, the upcoming 1964 election, and the president's impending trip to Dallas. Bill was back in Ghana when the news of the assassination came over the wire. His life would never be the same. A friend later told him that when LBJ was going over a list of Kennedy appointments and came to the name of the man who had turned the Arizona delegation from Johnson to Kennedy in 1960, LBJ said, "Who is this Irish SOB?"

A distaste for LBJ may have been the only political concept that Richard Kleindienst and Bill Mahoney shared. In the period after the 1964 election, Richard Nixon came back to Arizona. Richard Kleindienst had met then-Vice President Nixon during the 1956 Arizona Republican Convention, where Kleindienst was elected chairman. Afterward, during the drive to the airport, the Vice President turned to Kleindienst and said, "Dick, from now on, you're my man in Arizona."[33] Kleindienst had had his fill of losing campaigns, and although the idea of a Nixon comeback seemed the longest of long-shots in 1965, Kleindienst had to admire Nixon's determination to win back an election many Republicans thought had been stolen from them in 1960.

November 1968 must have been an especially sweet time for Richard Kleindienst. Barry Goldwater's landslide loss to Lyndon Johnson had been replaced by Richard Nixon completing his political comeback. In early 1969, President Nixon's "man in Arizona" was invited to Washington to become deputy attorney general. He was widely admired by the United States attorneys who served during his term as deputy and, later, attorney general. H.M. Ray, who served as a U.S. attorney in both the Kennedy-Johnson and Nixon-Ford years, thought Kleindienst was the best friend the U.S. attorneys had in Washington. When Attorney General John Mitchell stepped down to run President Nixon's reelection campaign in 1972, Richard Kleindienst, the former honor student and student body president of Winslow High School, became the Attorney General of the United States. One of the first things he did, of course, was to invite Miss Oare to visit him in Washington.

Richard Kleindienst's career as attorney general was at once difficult and short, both largely because of the man in the White House. When he was deputy attorney general, Nixon called him personally and asked him to dump an antitrust case against a large Republican contributor. Kleindienst, furious, marched into John Mitchell's office and told him what had happened and that he would resign before doing something like that. Mitchell calmed him down: "Come on, you know Nixon. Half the time he says stuff he doesn't mean. I'll call him and tell him to forget it." Later Mitchell told Kleindienst that Nixon had agreed he was out of line and to forget that the conversation had ever occurred. At his confirmation hearings for attorney general, Kleindienst literally did that, responding in the negative to a question about attempted White House influence on the case.

President Nixon, who did Kleindienst no favor by calling him in the first place, put the knife in even deeper by announcing Kleindienst's resignation at the same time as that of Bob Halderman and John Ehrlichman, two White House aides deeply involved in

Watergate. In surely what must have been one of the most difficult moments of his life, Richard Kleindienst found himself entering a guilty plea to a misdemeanor for his inaccurate response to congressional questions about President Nixon's call.[34]

Richard Nixon resigned in 1974 and Richard Kleindienst returned to the practice of law only to find himself embroiled in another crisis. Together with a Phoenix law firm, he represented a group of investors wishing to purchase an insurance company. The head of the investor group turned out to be somewhat shady, and the group eventually went into receivership. Arizona insurance regulators sought to recover the fee paid to the lawyers. An ethics complaint ensued, and, in the course of the investigation by the Bar, Kleindienst provided some information that the Bar counsel thought was inaccurate. This led to criminal charges and a trial in Maricopa County.

Richard Kleindienst could not have been at a lower point in his life. I saw him at a restaurant in Phoenix during this period and went over to say hello, and he thanked me for coming over. The trial must have been pure agony for him—but one remarkable moment occurred when Mike Scott, Kleindienst's lawyer, called a character witness to the stand. "I have known Richard Kleindienst for forty years," said the witness in a strong and sure voice, "and although I cannot think of a single political idea of his that I ever agreed with, I think he is a completely honest and forthright man, and I cannot conceive of him knowingly committing perjury." I was not in that courtroom that day, but I am told that the eyes of Richard Kleindienst, WHS Class of 1941, welled up with tears as he looked at the witness, William P. Mahoney, WHS Class of 1934. Richard Kleindienst was acquitted on all counts.

I ran into Richard Kleindienst in Washington, D.C., after the 1976 election. I was there to attend the inauguration of President Carter and to celebrate my friend Dennis DeConcini's swearing-in as a United States senator. There was a small party in the senator's office and Richard was there. We reminisced about Winslow, the Mahoneys,[35] and the Kleindiensts.[36] We talked about his summer work in my father's service station and, of course, about Miss Oare, who had retired from teaching. We wondered what she might be doing, with no students to mentor and no debate teams to coach.

In 1988, I was in charge of a downtown Phoenix luncheon group that would invite speakers on topics of current interest. This was in the aftermath of a presidential election in which negative campaigning seemed to have reached a particularly low point. I contacted both of the major parties and invited them to suggest a speaker with some experience in national and state campaigns who could talk about campaign reform proposals. To my surprise, the Republican Party chose Richard Kleindienst and the Democrats chose Bill Mahoney. I thought a return surprise was in order, so I tracked down Miss Oare at a local rest home and arranged for her to be there. The Winslow Boys did a fine job in their presentations. I introduced everyone on the dais, except one. I could tell by the looks on the faces of those in the front rows that they were wondering who the trim elderly woman seated between our two speakers was. Finally, I introduced the teacher of the Winslow Boys, all of us.

Epilogue

Thinking I was done with the Winslow Boys, quite by accident, I met another. Back in town for an all-class reunion, I went down to the hotel lobby for coffee and a Sunday newspaper and met Mitsubishi Nomoto. Neither a lawyer nor a politician, he had many of the same memories of growing up in the same small-town environment. He knew both of their elders. Al Kleindienst was a favorite of the Nomoto family, often visiting them during the holidays. Bill Mahoney, Sr. was in charge of the Santa Fe Railroad police and the largely Japanese American locomotive mechanics. His father, Kenzi, knew and respected the elder Mahoney's even-handed approach to railway security.

Everyone in town called my coffee companion "Mits," and it stuck. Born in Winslow in 1924, he and his sisters attended its public schools for two decades. He was in the Class of 1942, one year behind Richard Kleindienst. In his sophomore year, he worked on Richard's successful campaign for student body president. "By one vote," Mits would remind his friend, who would later become United States Attorney General. "Mine!"

"I did not graduate with my class," Mits told me as we sat there. The moment he said that I had a sinking feeling about the reason but was not about to interrupt his story. He then took me back to the fall of 1941, when he had begun his senior year at Winslow High School.

Like the other Winslow Boys, he took American government from Miss Oare. He loved the subject matter and was impressed by her obvious passion for the Constitution and the Bill of Rights. Mits reveled in the thought of these rights. He would pepper Miss Oare with questions, in and after class. To have lit such an inquisitive flame is something every teacher dreams of, and she treated his questions with care and deliberation. He could not wait to go home in the evenings to tell his parents, first-generation immigrants, about the wonders of their adopted land and the way in which it valued the rights of the individual.

One Saturday morning in the winter of his senior year, Mits checked in at the local Ford dealership for his regular part-time job. "I need you in early," his boss told him. "I just sold a used car over the phone to a man in Snowflake, and I need you to deliver it to him there." Mits loved this part of his job; it got him out of town and the chance to be by himself. His mother packed him a lunch that night and left it in the fridge for him.

The following day broke to a bitter wind sweeping over the two feet of snow that had fallen during the night. Mits bundled himself up, grabbed his lunch, and set out for Snowflake. The going was slippery and slow. Briefly stuck in a snowbank, he found some branches from a nearby tree to provide the traction to get unstuck. He arrived in the small Mormon community in time to catch the buyer as he was leaving for church. Passing on the keys and paperwork, Mits drove the man's trade-in vehicle back through Holbrook and into Winslow. The sun had turned the snow into slush, so the journey back went much quicker than the earlier ride.

Parking the trade-in next to the office, Mits strode into the boss' office. The look on the man's face was one of surprise, perhaps at how quickly the trip had turned around. "You're fired," said his boss in perfect deadpan. "Go straight home, do not stop on the way, and don't ever come back here again." Mits was stunned, but he knew the man was deadly serious. Something had gone wrong, terribly wrong, but this was no time to be asking questions.

At home, the window shades were drawn. The only sound was the radio blaring out the news: The armed forces of Japan had attacked the U.S. Naval Base at Pearl Harbor in the Hawaiian Islands, catching a number of battleships in port and dealing a terrible blow to American naval forces. The news had hardly sunk in when someone was knocking on the front door. This was not a polite knock or neighborly tap, but the bang of someone who might break the door down if not quickly answered. It was a city policeman, a young man the Nomoto family had known for years, who had waved them through intersections and smiled at them at school events, no longer smiling. "Do not leave this house without permission," he bellowed. "Your bank accounts are frozen, and you have no credit."

The Nomoto family—father Kenzi, mother Koume, sisters Kimito, Tazuko, and Patsy—lived in a two-story apartment building, owned by the Santa Fe Railroad, that was home to the families of men originally brought in to take the place of striking diesel mechanics. Fearful of the reaction of other railroad workers, who saw them as "strikebreakers," railroad officials provided the housing to keep the replacement workers close to their work and away from locals.

Kenzi Nomoto knew whom to call to bring some clarity to the alarming position his family found themselves in: He would call Al Kleindienst, Richard's father. "Big Al," as he was known at the Elks Club, was an imposing bear of a man, whose trademark was the big cigar, half-smoked and chewed to a frazzle, lodged in the corner of his mouth. His reputation was as simple as it was straightforward: If you were his friend, he could open doors for you. If not, look out. Mits listened in as his father pleaded with the senior Kleindienst: "This has to be for other people, those with sympathies to Japan. We are Americans. We love this country. My son would join the U.S. Army tomorrow if they would let him. Isn't there something you can do?" Mits could tell from the look on his father's face that the response was not helpful. "He told me to do what I was told and not to call him or try to talk to him ever again. He was cold, like someone who hated us."

Neither Mits nor his siblings were allowed to return to school. For the remainder of December, through January and into February, they were virtual prisoners in their own home. High school class-mates and teammates from football and basketball, like many in town, shunned them. There were exceptions. Mits's friend James Better and his family brought the Nomotos meals and companion-ship. Others, who valued friendship over peer pressure, helped the family: Ken Parker, Tom Keaton and Patsy Rhoton. It was a difficult and largely isolated time for the Nomotos and the other Japanese American families in their apartment building.

Finally came word that the families of Japanese in the smaller Arizona communities were to travel to Phoenix to report to a tem-porary relocation center. The Nomoto family dutifully packed up as much of their belongings that would fit in a car and left before dawn for the long drive. They would never see Winslow again. Mits did most of the driving, first retracing the delivery route to Snowflake he had made what seemed to be a lifetime ago. Down though Show Low, through the winding curves of the Salt River Canyon, through the mining communities of Globe, Miami, and Superior, and finally, in the late afternoon, to Phoenix.

When the Nomotos tried to find the address they had been given to report to, it turned out not to exist. There were six other families traveling in caravan with them, all growing concerned about where they would spend the night. Kenzi Nomoto remembered the name of Reverend Okomoto, a Methodist minister, whose Glendale church served a community of Japanese American families. Concerned for the safety of the Winslow group ("No Japs allowed" signs were popping up all over), Reverend Okomoto led the families to a building near his church and made makeshift beds in the hallway. He was also able to find out where they were to "report." Not Phoenix after all, but the small mining community of Mayer, closer to Prescott.

The Nomotos's stay in Mayer was brief; they soon found themselves relocated to Poston, a small community south of Parker on the Colorado River Indian Reservation near the Arizona-California border. A teenager at the time, who often drove families from the train station at Parker to the camp, describes the scene:

> Here were all these tarpaper shacks or barracks with double roofs on them, no vegetation, blowing dust, hot, like 110–115 degrees. Moving these people in there who essentially had their belongings on their back and in maybe one or two suitcases. Jamming them altogether in those barracks, destroying their whole way of life.

Mits was bored stiff in Poston. There was literally nothing to do and you could sweep out the barracks only so many times. When, six months into his stay there, camp officials announced there were mining and farming jobs in Colorado, Mits jumped at the chance. Following a long trip to Greeley, Colorado, Mits and his fellow internees were assigned to the sugar beet harvest. It was backbreaking work, constantly bending over and then standing up. One field he worked was near a German POW camp. He could hear them laughing, having meals, and playing soccer. The contrast between members of Adolf Hitler's armed forces, men whose job had been to kill Americans, was not lost on Mit. There was one bright spot to his experience: He met and later married Mary Oshima.

After the war ended, Mits and his family moved to California. They wanted no part of Arizona and the memories left behind. After they had settled down there, Mits sat down to write something he had been composing in his mind for years. The grammar would have to be perfect, his reflections on the Constitution careful and reasoned. The letter he would write would be to Miss Oare. She had taught him about the role of the Constitution and its protections against government overreaching. How, he would ask her, could a government be operating on that document and do what was done to families like his own, whose "crime" was to be of Japanese descent? He was sure Miss Oare would have an answer; she would be able to explain what had happened to the Nomotos and what part of the Constitution it was based on. He sent the letter. Surely, she would respond. He waited, checking the mailbox every day. The days turned to weeks, the weeks to months.

In fairness to Miss Oare, there is no way to know if she ever received the letter, so we cannot know if her lack of response was intentional. Had she responded, she might have told Mits that a 1944 Supreme Court decision found justification for implementation of the practice based on the military threat to the West Coast of the United States following Pearl Harbor; but, in a companion case, found unconstitutional the continued internment of American citizens as to whom there was no proof of disloyalty.

In 1992, Mits attended the fiftieth reunion of the high school class he was not permitted to graduate from. He bumped into his old friend James Betters. They had been corresponding over the years. They talked about President Roosevelt's executive order; how West Coast cities felt particularly vulnerable to Japanese attack and the inconsistent way in which internment was carried out. Jim was not sure how to answer these questions, but he had an idea who might be able to, for Richard Kleindienst, the former attorney general of the United States, was at the reunion. Richard was delighted to see old friends and greeted them with a warm handshake. They talked about the people of Winslow they had grown up with and around. Mits reminded Richard that he had once said to him, "Someday, you may be able to vote for me for President." "Well," Mits said, "you came pretty close." "Too damned close, some might say," Richard responded.

Finally, Mits asked how it came to be that his family was essentially run out of town. Through misty eyes, Richard admitted what he had told few others, that his own father was part of the group responsible for the knock on the Nomotos's door some fifty years back. There was apparently concern among railroad officials that a vital line of supplies for the war effort might be in danger if Japanese Americans were allowed to work on the locomotives. "I told Dad that was wrong and what they did made them no better than the mob that threatened our family on election night in 1936."

Mits remembered Christmas of 1940. His father had made a pen-and-ink drawing especially for their Kleindienst neighbors, wrapped up carefully and presented on behalf of all Japanese American railroad workers. As Mits listened to Richard speak, Mits bowed his head. Not out of sadness for the discovery of an ancient perfidy, but out of respect for an old friend who had done a great favor—telling the truth when painful to do so. He looked his old friend in the eye and said: "I'm still glad I voted the way I did."

Officers of Winslow, Arizona Elks Club, circa 1956. Front row center is Leo Lewis (The Flournoy Fireplug); to his left is William Bert Hawkins (author's father). In the second row, second person from the left is Al Kleindienst.

GOING HOME

I'm standin' on a corner in Winslow, Arizona
Such a fine sight to see[37]

It sits in a saucer-like dish in the middle of the Colorado Plateau, looking across the always muddy Little Colorado River and into the always beautiful Painted Desert. First, last, and foremost a railroad town, it was originally located where it is (instead of the more scenic Sunset Pass twenty miles to the south) because of the availability of Clear Creek's steady supply of water for the Santa Fe steam engines of the late 1800s.

Its heyday was just after World War II. Its airport—built up to land troop supplies—was one of the busiest in the state. Until the mid-1950s, even TWA flew regular flights in and out. In its very early days, it had an opera house, and Hollywood celebrities would stop to entertain the locals while trains were fueled and cleaned. Some would stay at La Posada Hotel and dine in the Turquoise Room, waited on by Harvey Girls. The 1950 census showed 8,500 residents. Not bad when you consider that Phoenix was then a sleepy town of 45,000.

Today, it is not much more than 8,000. Although the hope of locals that a state prison complex might bring some of its professional staff to town (they wound up commuting from Flagstaff) didn't pan out,

HGTV recently featured it as part of their "Hometown" series, which resulted in the remodel of the root beer stand where Phyllis once worked. Still, a town that has produced war heroes (my baseball coach, Jay Vargas—a Vietnam Congressional Medal of Honor winner), an ambassador (William P. Mahoney—John F. Kennedy's ambassador to Ghana), and a United States Attorney General (Richard Nixon's Richard Kleindienst) cannot be easily discounted or quickly forgotten.

It was a substantial mystery to our son Adam in his youth. How, he marveled, can people who have never met him walk up to him and say: "You're Adam Hawkins, aren't you?" When a teenager, son Aaron thought it something of a Humphrey Bogart movie—black and white and from a distant past when television didn't even exist.

More recently, one of Phyllis's cousins, who had never been to Winslow before, stopped in a store and struck up this conversation:

Cousin Steve: My uncle was a doctor here years ago.

Clerk: What was his name?

Steve: Leo Lewis.

Clerk: He delivered me.

Until the mid-1950s, television did not exist in Winslow. On cool summer evenings, the preferred activity was a long walk—up Williamson, across Aspinwall, down Kinsley, past porches with people in swings and rockers. And there was always time for a chat: "Hear the Lacey boy is quite a pitcher—Notre Dame may even want him."

Although nearly two thousand feet lower, Winslow often manages winters colder than Flagstaff, its more prosperous rival to the west.[38] January would bring a depressing fog, which would hang over the town like a frozen blanket. My high school buddy Jon Grove (who became the chief financial officer of a major development company) would make a foghorn-like sound: "B…O…R…I…N…G." Competition for the high school basketball team, as a result, was ferocious—making it meant, after all, one, maybe two trips to Phoenix. I never made it, but my buddy Dee Martin did and dutifully reported, upon his return, that there really was a sun.

Until we lost her, we would go back to see my mother, visit old friends, and marvel at how little it had really changed. It has a marvelous leveling effect. "Take it easy," as the Eagles advised, "don't let the sound of your own wheels drive you crazy."

Little things confirm its unchanging nature. We took the boys to the Tonto Drive-In Theater. The best speakers were still up front. "The movie never starts on time," Phyllis predicted to the boys. "Twenty minutes after it was supposed to start, everyone will honk their horns and then it will start." Her memories of 1963 (Troy Donahue and Sandra Dee in *A Summer Place*) proved absolutely reliable predictors that at least one train would pass by in the middle of the movie. There were two. Progress, I suppose.

In truth, it was a marvelous place to grow up. Black, brown, red, and white all went to the same high school and played on the same teams. We were all Bulldogs, and the most important colors were maroon and white. It was also an environment of patriotism and orderliness, but yet a knowing understanding of and tolerance for the excesses of youth. A community where teachers were considered important citizens, it was (and is) not unusual for high school graduations to draw half the adult population to watch the town's best pass into adulthood.

Thomas Wolfe may well be right in observing that you can never go home. Maybe you can simply visit, look around, and reflect on the many people who made up the fabric of the town. I have been to Ashville, North Carolina, Wolfe's hometown, which is a wonderful place, but I cannot imagine it could have been a better place to grow up than the little town of my youth.

ROBBIE BROWN

A recent magazine piece featured a series of pieces about those who had served in Vietnam during hostilities there. They got me to thinking about those who did not return. I had heard that a classmate, Robbie Brown, was one, but I was not sure.

Robert Brown
WHS Class of 1963

My brother alerted me to a website that lists Vietnam casualties by their hometown. Now I could find out about Robbie for sure. Scrolling down to the town of our youth—Winslow, Arizona—there were familiar names: Albert Chavez and Jimmy Schibi. But no Robbie Brown. The site also contained an alphabetical list, so it was time to be sure. The thing that strikes you in doing this is the number of lost lives: 618 from Arizona alone. Finally, down at the bottom of the Bs, there he was: Robert Alva Brown II, listing Needles, California, apparently the place where he received his draft notice. Pictured is his senior class photo, frozen in time and displaying a smile that would light up a room.

Robbie and I were born in Winslow two weeks apart in February 1945. We attended the same elementary, middle, and high school. When we were both about seven, we would ride our Schwinns to the edge of town and imagine that the Korean War was happening just over the horizon.

In September 1968, when I was starting my second year of law school and a year and a half from returning to active duty with the Marines, Robbie Brown, now a U.S. Army sergeant, was leading a patrol in Vietnam's Hua Nghia province, near the village of Cu Cui. When his troops encountered enemy fire, he directed his men to flank the source of the opposing fire. In the process of supplying his troops with ammunition and leading a charge against a fortified bunker, he was cut down himself, mortally wounded on a battlefield that would take the lives of some fifty thousand Americans. For his conspicuous bravery, Robbie was awarded the Distinguished Service Cross, the Army's second-highest award for valor.

Robbie was a good student in high school, the vice president of both our freshman and senior classes, and an active athlete, playing football, baseball, and track. He combined the latter two his senior year, something of a unique combination as the two sports practiced at the same time. He particularly excelled in wrestling, serving as team captain and finishing second in the state in his weight class (138 pounds). Active in school clubs (Future Teachers, Quill & Scroll), he even played in the band during his freshman year.

While other conflicts have drawn our attention lately, Vietnam was the defining moment in the lives of our generation. For men ages eighteen to twenty-six, military conscription, the Draft, was staring you right in the face. According to Ed Buford, Robbie's Army buddy in infantry training at Fort Polk, Louisiana, both he and Robbie were against the war, but they nonetheless went into the Army when their Draft letters arrived.

A war that Vietnamese refer to as "the American War" lasted in earnest for the last half of the 1960s and into the early 1970s. America's relations with Vietnam are entirely different now with the two countries having recently entered into a bilateral trade agreement. The Domino Theory, which fired up supporters of the war—the idea that the loss of South Vietnam would inevitably lead to China's domination of the region—has now given way to Vietnam being seen as a valued trading partner and a checkpoint to Beijing's domination of South Asia.

But the impact on individual lives is not part of the calculus of foreign policy. In the snap of an instant, a life full of promise can be gone forever. By the time I returned to active duty, the Marines were largely out of Vietnam, but men I had gone through officer boot camp with had come back bearing scars both physical and mental. And some, like Robbie Brown, came back only to be buried in hometown graveyards, in his case Desert View Cemetery in the little town of our youth. His name can be found on the Vietnam Veterans Memorial Wall in Washington, D.C. (Wall 43, line 45).

Epilogue

The original circulation of this story to friends and family brought considerable comment. Ed Novak, recipient of the Silver Star for valor in Vietnam, stated simply: "I liked your Robbie Brown." Issac Bonds, two years behind Robbie and me in high school and easily the best basketball player in Winslow history: "Your letter touched me in quite a few ways. As a Vietnam veteran myself it brought back memories that I have tried to bury for years. I was one of the fortunate to return without very many physical scars but many, many emotional and mental scars. Some I'm dealing with until this day." Issac underwent psychological counseling, learning the meaning of survivor's guilt. He knew Robbie and that he was a strong person. Issac also knew others who did not come home and some who took their own lives after coming home. He has now found comfort in his faith.

HERB

Lewis Herbert Renfro was the first black adult I ever knew. He was a big man with huge hands, which must have seemed larger to a sixteen-year-old than they really were, but they were still big.

He worked for the railroad, as almost everyone in Winslow did. He was a Pullman porter, a service position, on trains that headed either east to Gallup or west to Barstow. Years later, his son, the fleet halfback on our football team, became an engineer, having moved all the way from the back of the bus to driving the train.

He could quote the Bible as floridly as any person I've ever known. Unlike the scolding of television preachers of the day, his Bible was a gentle, forgiving vehicle. He knew all the spiritual hymns. "Amazing grace," his sweet voice would flow forward, "that saved a wretch like me." I cannot hear that hymn today without thinking of him.

He had a sideline: making tamales, good, thick pasty masa with lots of meat and chili. He would sell them in his spare time, walking up and down First Street, greeting the people he knew, which seemed to be practically everyone.

He would stop by my dad's gas station on long summer evenings when I was working the late shift, catching the last travelers of the day trying to make it the final sixty miles to Flagstaff before they stopped for the night. We would talk about life, people, and the events of the day. He was exceptionally well read, when I think back about our conversations. I imagine him having slipped a book or two into his bag when he rode the rails. He could bring you out with a simple question: "What do you suppose is going on over there in Selma, Alabama?" Later, as a sophomore in college, in the aftermath of the Sunday Massacre on the Edmund Pettis Bridge, I knew exactly who Sheriff Jim Clark was when the dean of students invited him to speak on campus.

Herb could laugh—God he could laugh. The kind of laughter that makes you feel good just to hear it, that embraces and makes you feel a part of the joy that produced it. He saw great changes in our little town and the world around it: the public swimming pool desegregated; the "whites only" seating at the movie theater discarded.

One June night in the 1970s, I drove back to the little town of my youth, this time to speak to the graduating seniors. I was the United States Attorney for Arizona at the time and had given dozens of speeches; this one was different. These were the people who knew me "when." On the drive up, I rehearsed the speech over and over so that every word would be precise—after all, my English teachers would be in the audience. High school graduation in Winslow was a big event, filling the football stadium with more than just the parents of the graduates. I wanted to show the people that their patience and tolerance of a somewhat wild kid was a good investment.

As I got out of the car and started to walk in, I saw him walking up. We hadn't seen each other in years, and I felt bad for not keeping in touch. He swept all that away in a moment. Turning up the collar of my jacket with one hand and holding me by my shoulders, my old friend of tamales and summer talks looked in the eye of the rough-edged kid now looking every bit the part of a big city lawyer and said: "You tell 'em, Mister Mike, you tell 'em."

HALE FELLOW

He had, by all accounts, a truly sparkling personality, the kind of person who could light up a room just by being there. And yet, there was something slightly contradictory about him, as if there was a darkness below all the sparkle. It was not noticeable at first; you had to be around him long enough to get past the quick hellos and how-are-yous. Past the questions about your parents, the kind of small talk politicians are so good at. Once there, you could sense he really wanted to open up and maybe tell you how his own life was as frustrating or deeply unrewarding as your own sometimes seemed to be. He was the first to buy a round of drinks and often the last to leave when the bar closed down. His wife was attractive and well-dressed, their children freshly scrubbed and polite. In a town of relative sameness, where everyone worked for or because of the railroad, his position stood out: bank president.

No one seemed to know a whole lot about where he was from. A big city, maybe, someplace with lots of goings-on. But no one doubted where he was headed, and that was up. Phyllis met him when she was lifeguarding in the country club pool. She had the impression they would not be caught dead at the public pool. "You should have seen him," as I half-listened to her while also listening to Vin Scully describe the efforts of the Dodgers to win on a night when neither Sandy Koufax nor Don Drysdale were pitching. "He just swaggered into the room and bought drinks for everyone at the bar. But there is just something about him, something that you can't put your finger on." Turning the car radio off, I said: "Maybe he's just an arrogant jerk."

"No, silly, there's something about him that just doesn't make sense, an anger, a frustration, something." I could sense that making out was now out of the question as Phyllis was deep in thought. I made a mental note to write to Dodgers manager Walter Alston with my thoughts on improving the team.

And then one summer morning, he kissed his wife and kids and drove to Phoenix, to another bank. The headlines the next day somehow made everything fall into place: "Small Town Bank President Arrested in Holdup Attempt." It turned out he was an awful bank robber. Driving up to the teller window and handing the obligatory note, she asked him to wait, and he did, just long enough to see an off-duty police officer approaching with a drawn pistol. It was as if he wanted to be caught, as if the dark side of him was crying out for help. And he left the people in our town with stories that began with: "You know there was just something about that guy that didn't make sense."

THE FLOURNOY FIREPLUG

It is 1918. The twentieth century is still a teenager. Woodrow Wilson, in the fifth year of his presidency, is extolling a disinterested Congress to extend the right to vote to women. Although the President is but a year away from winning the Nobel Peace Prize, World War I is raging in Europe. Germany, having made its peace with Russia, is massing its forces against those of Britain, France, and the United States on the Western Front. The national college football championship goes to the University of Pittsburgh with a record of four wins and one loss. The Rose Bowl is a contest between the Mare Island Marines and an Army squad from Camp Lewis. (The Marines win, of course, 19–7.) The Metropolitan Opera showcases the world premiere of *Il Trittico*, a series of three one-act operas by Giacomo Puccini. The American Railroad Express Company is formed under federal supervision by the enforced merger of the Adams, American, Wells Fargo, and Southern Express Companies. The drought between World Series wins for the Chicago Cubs is extended to ten years, with the Boston Red Sox winning what would prove to be their last World Series of the twentieth century, defeating the Cubs four games to two.[39]

In a mostly Italian American neighborhood on the near west side of Chicago is a growing family in a small house at 1419 West Flournoy Street. Actually, "small" does not begin to describe the size of the Lewis home. The Bunicontros, their neighbors in the flat next door, would pound on the wall, and the Lewises knew to open their window and reach out for a plate of spaghetti or ravioli. This episode, which would repeat itself regularly, reveals something more than the close-built nature of the neighborhood: Abraham and Sarah Lewis and their children may have been the only Jewish family in the neighborhood, but their neighbors treated them with compassion and respect.

On May 4, 1918, there was a new arrival in the Lewis home, Leo Lester Lewis, the fifth of what would be six children. Although the home was near Cook County Hospital, the family could not afford the luxury of a hospital birth. Leo joined his older sisters Ann, Lilian, and Gladys and older brother Sam. Sister Silvia (known to this day as Babe) would come along in the next two years. This was long before the widespread availability of birth control[40] and a new baby was a regular event. The family might have been larger—Sarah suffered one or two miscarriages and at least one infant death.

The mother was Sarah Esther Lewis, who had immigrated from what is now Lithuania. Her family name before Ellis Island was Kuklansky; Immigration authorities thought "Cook" sounded better. She had a brother, Hyman, who lived in El Dorado, Kansas, and came to Chicago once a year. A favorite of Leo's, Uncle Hy had a metal recycling business in Kansas. Sarah also had a brother, Joseph, who lived on the far west side of Chicago and was married to Aunt Esther. Esther, something of a scold, was particularly frightening to the meek and quiet Sarah.

"Ma," as Leo called her, was a good cook, someone who could make something out of nothing. If necessity is the mother of invention, then Sarah Lewis was the Thomas Edison of the kitchen. Lentil, cabbage, and, of course, chicken soup, were common fare. She made her own noodles and plucked her own chickens. Circumstances and tradition made her old-fashioned; the house had no refrigerator and used a pot-bellied stove for heating. On cold winter evenings, the kids would crowd around the stove for warmth. When older sister

Lil got a job, she bought the family its first refrigerator and heater. Sarah's efforts to keep a kosher kitchen were challenged by the times. Leo recalls a barrel in which the Passover dishes were kept, but the Depression saw them scatter to the families of the children.

The family lost their father very early. Leo was just six and Babe four when their father, Abraham Lester Lewis, passed away. Like Sarah, an immigrant from Eastern Europe, there is something of an air of mystery about Abraham to this day. We know he was quite young, forty-eight years, when he died of pulmonary tuberculosis. This was not a sudden death; Abraham had fought TB for years and even spent time in a Denver hospital. He made a living supplying local grocers with fruit and vegetables, making ample use of his horse and buggy. Abraham also made a living on the side as a bootlegger. Leo recalls going in the attic one day and seeing a contraption with "lots of coils and steam."[41] The end product (and just how Leo knows this we will leave to speculation) was mead—a strong fermented fruit drink, popular with European immigrants of the day.

The Lewis children, Leo included, went to neighborhood public schools: John McLaren Grammar School and Cregier Junior High School. Leo quickly developed a reputation as an excellent student, a reputation that placed higher expectations on the family members who followed. "It was very difficult to perform to his standards," recalled Babe, who was two years behind. Leo attended the neighborhood high school, Richard T. Crane Technical High. It was known as a "plumber's school"—one where plumbing would be the highest expected career goal of most of its students. Whatever else high school gave him, his sisters recall Leo as an excellent handyman, someone who could fix just about anything.

The handyman reputation got around to the neighbors. On one hot summer day, the local kids implored Leo to "open" the fire hydrant so they could romp in the cool spray. Leo finally gave in, borrowed a monkey wrench, and just as he began to loosen the top bolt, a Chicago police officer grabbed Leo and took him to the

Maxwell Street Police Station. The same kids who had egged Leo on now pointed fingers at him. When Babe ran in to tell her mother what had happened, she said, "Good; he can cool off in jail." At the station house, a ruddy-faced desk sergeant explained to Leo how what he was trying to do could endanger public safety by lowering water pressure at other fire hydrants. The lecture made sense to the aspiring engineering student; he never tried again.

More than a handyman, Leo was also something of an artist. Babe fondly remembers a pencil drawing of Mickey Mouse that he drew for her. When he later had children of his own, Leo amazed them by painting cartoon figures on the wall of the backyard. Where the other houses had wood fences or bland brick, the Lewises had lions, tigers, and bears. That talent surfaced in his grandson Aaron, whose drawings of automobiles on homework bedeviled his teachers, but now delight his superiors at Central Stile of Fiat Motor Company in Turin, Italy.

Leo's pre-teenage youth was spent in the Chicago of the 1920s. Alphonse "Al" Capone was boss of the Chicago underworld at that time and violence was never very far away. Leo was sitting on his front stoop one evening when a car drove by and an occupant of the vehicle shot a man on the other side of the street. The man was dead before anyone could reach him. Although the street was crawling with people, several of them much closer to the event than Leo, "no one saw anything."

All of the Lewises worked and contributed to the well-being of the family. Sisters Ann and Gladys worked at Western Union Telegraph Company. "Ann was a crack stenographer," Leo remembers. "She could take it down as fast as anyone could talk it." Lilian went to nursing school and worked at Westside Hospital. Babe worked as a legal secretary. Brother Sam worked part-time in Sam Solomon's drugstore, while earning a degree in pharmacy.

Leo began working at about the age of ten and had a constant stream of jobs. He started as a delivery boy for a drugstore, a job his brother Sam had before him. "Whenever he got out of one job, I took what he had left behind." After school and in the evenings, he sold newspapers at a downtown newsstand. On weekends, he would peddle papers and cigarettes at a kiosk at Union Station. The newsstand was bitter-cold work in Chicago's winters. The trucks delivering the newspapers to the newsstand would roar around the corner and spit out a stack of bound newspapers. Half the time, the papers would fall "kerplunk" in the water.

Leo's work at the newsstand was in the day of widespread newspaper competition, and Chicago had several dailies. Leo sold them all—William Randolph Hearst's *Evening American* and *Herald American* and Robert R. McCormick's *Chicago Tribune*. Even Marshall Field of department store fame put out a newspaper, called *PM*. Leo remembers its distinctive size—about half that of other newspapers: "It was a sensible size. You could fold it out and still read on a street-car or a bus without bothering people around you." Leo would have been sixteen and still selling newspapers on January 30, 1934, when the world learned of the appointment of Adolf Hitler as chancellor of Germany.

The *Chicago Tribune* sponsored a typesetting contest at about this time. First prize was a job, and so Leo was eager to enter. He won and reported for work in a large, cavernous room lit with a distinctive green light—an atmosphere more like a morgue. He was apprehensive enough when he sat down at a typesetting machine, only to feel a warm breath on the back of his neck. Frightened, but afraid to show it, he whipped around and shouted: "Get away from me!" The problem was that the person he had just shouted at was Mr. Walscheimer, the head typesetter, who simply wanted to look over the shoulder of his newest employee. Leo knew what was coming next, so he picked up his pink slip, ending his typesetting career before it ever really began.

While still in high school, Leo landed a job with the Railway Express Company at Chicago's Union Station. The work put him outside and exposed to the elements. His most persistent memory is that of the wind coming in off Lake Michigan. "God, was it cold; I wore two pairs of gloves most of the time." The job required him to load and unload the trucks that pulled into the docks. Eventually, he was promoted to the position of router. This required him to mark packages with the proper train for the intended destination. They gave him a big book with all the various routes and trains in it—but he quickly realized he would have to memorize the information in the book. "The packages moved so quickly and there was so much to do, if you hesitated, you were lost." All of the trains came into Chicago in those days: the Great Northern, the Union Pacific, and the Atchison, Topeka, and Santa Fe. He had no way of knowing it at the time, but the Santa Fe Railroad would play a large role in his later life.

At this point, the high school student with the quick mind and good memory became a union member. This was not a matter of prior planning. A union boss came around and asked him if he would "like" to join the Brotherhood of Railroad Platformmen & Baggage Handlers. When Leo told the man he could not afford to join, he was told he couldn't afford not to. "He made it clear that if I refused, my time card would be pulled. Without that, I simply could not work." Leo still has that union card. The job lasted through high school and junior college.

Herzl Junior College, on Independence Boulevard near Douglas Park, was Leo's next stop. He wanted very much to be an engineer, but the math proved to be insurmountable. "Calculus and algebra were one thing, but when we got to differential equations and quantum mechanics, I knew I was in over my head." What may have also helped discourage him was learning that the greatest demand for engineering graduates was overseas, and this was a precarious time to be traveling, especially for a young Jewish kid from Chicago. A fellow student—Leo remembers him as bright and idealistic—suggested medicine, joking, "You know, they allow Jews to become doctors."[42] The idea was intriguing to Leo, so he switched to a pre-medical course of study, went to summer school, and took extra courses to prepare for medical school.

Fully expecting not to be admitted on his first try, Leo was surprised when the acceptance letter came in the mail from the University of Illinois. Although its main campus was downstate in Champagne-Urbana, the Illinois Medical School was in Chicago. Like many of the schools he had attended earlier, the medical school was within walking distance of the house on Flournoy. He was all of twenty years when he entered medical school in the fall of 1939.

It was, to put it mildly, an extraordinarily uncertain time. The effects of the Depression ("We were so poor, I'm not sure we noticed it") had yet to wear off. In January 1939, Adolf Hitler, in a speech widely reported in American newspapers, announced that if war broke out, it would mean extermination for the Jews of Europe. On September 1, 1939, German troops invaded Poland. Three months later, midway through Leo's medical studies, came the Japanese attack on Pearl Harbor. Like many of his classmates, Leo applied for a reserve commission in the U.S. Army. There was now no mystery as to what he would be doing upon graduation.

Leo loved medical school. The class consisted of 143 students, one of the largest medical school classes in the country at the time. Among his classmates were one African American man and "one or two" women. "Women now make up a majority of entering medical students," Leo, the prolific reader, now observes. "And, they make really good doctors."

What others found boring or challenging, he found exciting and adventuresome. Some cringed at the sight of blood or cadavers. Leo couldn't get enough of his surgery and anatomy classes. Like the schools he had attended earlier, the medical school was within walking distance of Sarah Lewis's kitchen. A collapsed wartime schedule allowed him to complete his formal studies in three and one-half years. In March 1943, at the same time German troops were liquidating the Krakow ghetto in Poland, Leo Lewis—the neighbor-hood handyman and newspaper vendor—became Doctor Leo Lewis.

Attending medical school did not put an end to the need to work. Leo spent his afternoons working the soda fountain and helping out with prescriptions at a drugstore owned by his brother-in-law Sam Solomon. Sam had married Leo's sister Ann. One afternoon, a thin, extremely attractive young woman—he would later learn she was a model—came in the drugstore. He had never seen anyone like her: hazel-eyed and blonde with a Southern drawl you could cut with a knife. She sat down at the counter and asked for a Dr Pepper. It was like asking for a Yoo-hoo in Atlanta. He had no idea what she was talking about. "Would a Coke do?" She laughed and said, "Sure." He was clearly smitten with her and prayed this was not her last visit. When Lois Newman returned a few days later, Leo screwed up the courage to ask her out, and somewhat to his surprise, she agreed.

We have a photograph of the two of them taken at about this time. They are standing at a guardrail on a boat on Lake Michigan. She has a dazzling smile and the high cheekbones that show today in granddaughters she would never see. He is thin, dark-haired, staring out through round-rimmed sunglasses that have come back into fashion. If you did not know them and someone told you they were movie stars, you would not have blinked an eye.

Lois Newman was all of eighteen when she met Leo Lewis, the soda jerk and doctor-to-be. Born in rural South Carolina, she had grown up in Anderson, "just down the road from Clemson," as she would say. To describe her as headstrong and impulsive would be a serious understatement. From about sixteen on, she suffered from serious wanderlust. She had had enough of the sleepy South; the big city was calling, and she was listening. She had tried to leave home one year earlier, only to be pulled back by her stern papa. At the time she met Leo, she was visiting her Aunt Montie, a telephone operator who lived in the same neighborhood as the drugstore.

Leo did not bring Lois home at first. His brother Sam had married outside the family faith and, although she never said a word, Leo had sensed his mother's deep disappointment. His fears, it turned out, were overblown. Although this Deep South Baptist could not have been more different, everyone in the family instantly liked her. "It was hard not to like her," recalls Babe. "She was full of life and had a way of making you feel comfortable around her." They could also sense something else. The pressure of performing in school and the constant demanding work had made Leo subject to depression. Lois lifted his spirits and made him laugh. She could tease him where others could not—"Polecat" she would call him. She was pure tonic for him, an elixir that made him whole.

In 1942, during his third year of medical school, they slipped over to Davenport, Iowa, to get married. "The quick marriage capital of the Midwest," Leo recalls. They lived in an apartment on the near north side, on Oak Street. Lois had been living at the Girls Friendly Society. They did not, as Lois would observe later, "have two rocks to rub together," but they were deliriously happy.

Following an internship at Grant Hospital, Leo accepted his reserve commission in the U.S. Army Medical Corps. There is a home movie taken about this time. In it, an adoring family surrounds Leo in his Army uniform. Lois, Leo's sisters, and a young Sam Solomon all appear.

There is an unmistakable gleam of pride in everyone's eyes. In a brief moment of time, with a war raging in Europe and rumors of the darkest of evils beginning to circulate, this close-knit family, the sons and daughters of immigrants who had grown up in what can only be called desperate poverty, took time to share in the accomplishments of their brother and their own contributions to it. The smallish, bright-eyed Jewish kid from the near west side of Chicago, the newspaper boy and baggage handler, was now Doctor Lewis and about to become Captain Lewis. He had a beautiful new wife who would soon bring him a daughter. Leo must have felt as close to heaven as he could ever imagine. He was about to see a large slice of hell.

Now officially in the military, Leo's first stop was six weeks at Carlysle Barracks in Pennsylvania for Medical Field Training School. From there, a brief stop in Charleston, South Carolina, and then on to Camp Chafee in the town of Fort Smith, Arkansas. Leo sweltered in the Arkansas heat, but Lois felt right at home.

In November 1944, following a romantic weekend with Lois, Leo shipped out of New York for Europe on a "Victory" ship. These small, maneuverable vessels traveled in a convoy—zigzagging across the North Atlantic to avoid German U-boats. In December 1944, Leo's ship arrived in Le Havre, on the northwest coast of France.

It had been six months since the D-Day landing, and Allied forces had extended the front line to a point running southeast from Dunkirk to the Saar region on the border between France and Germany. The U.S. Third Army, under the command of General George S. Patton, was pushing its way toward the Rhine River. The crossing of the Rhine, replete with the image of General Patton urinating into it from a pontoon bridge, was considered the symbol of the beginning of the end for German forces.[43]

In Europe at last, Leo was given command of a Medical Collecting Company attached to Patton's Third Army. It was a command by default; the only other doctor in the company was one month junior in rank. This was a war in which the Medical Corps played an extraordinary role. For the wounded who made it to an aid station or a field hospital, the chances for survival were a remarkable 98 percent. This had a profound impact on the frontline troops. "We were convinced that the Army had a regulation against dying in an aid station," remarked one frontline officer.[44]

A series of photographs shows Captain Leo Lewis at various points along the route of Patton's march to the Rhine: an overnight stay in a chateau once belonging to a French collaborator in Forges

Les Eur, a weary-looking Leo enjoying a smoke after a long day at a battalion aid station just inside Germany, a World War I monument in Haar, Germany, and sitting in his Jeep at a POW clearing camp in Konstantinbad, Czechoslovakia, in the Sudetenland.

Patton's army was legendary for the speed at which it traveled, and the constant demands placed on his troops. During the day, they rocketed through France, across the southern tip of Germany, and into Czechoslovakia. Each night, General Patton wanted every piece of equipment on the ground and in place, only to be packed up the next morning to move on. This meant that the Medical Corps would have to set up an entire field hospital each night only to tear it down in the morning. Leo finally talked to Patton's chief of staff and worked out an arrangement where the medical tents would be put up, but only that equipment necessary to that evening's work unloaded.

Patton, as was his wont, arrived in Prague weeks prior to the arrival of Russian troops. Leo recalls Prague as a beautiful city, but his stay there was short-lived. Prague was in what was to be the Soviet Sector, and Patton was ordered to pull back to Pilsen, a beautiful town in the Czech countryside famous for Budenweisen, the original Budweiser beer.

It was now March 1945. The German war machine was on its last legs; Russian forces were pressing from the East and Allied forces from the West. Still, Hitler pushed forward with plans to eradicate the Jews of Europe. January had seen the death march of prisoners out of Auschwitz and Stutthof. In March, the inmates of Buchenwald were marched out, many to their death.

On April 30, 1945, Third Army forces reached Landsberg in the foothills of the German Alps and encountered their first concentration camp. Part of the Dachau complex, this was not an extermination camp, but a work camp designed to produce war goods. Nevertheless, the Americans were horrified by what they saw: prisoners, by the hundreds, in striped pajamas, three-quarters starved, corpses, little more than skeletons, by the thousands. An Army officer recalled his reaction:

> The memory of starved, dazed men, who dropped their eyes and heads when we looked at them through the chain-link fence, in the same manner that a beaten, mistreated dog would cringe, leaves feelings that cannot be described and will never be forgotten. The impact of seeing those people left me saying, only to myself, "Now I know why I am here."[45]

The scene so infuriated General Maxwell Taylor that he declared martial law and ordered the citizens of Landsberg, from fourteen to eighty years, out of their homes and marched to the camp. With rakes, brooms, and shovels, they buried the bodies and cleaned the camp. On the march back to town, many were still vomiting.[46]

Landsberg would become Leo's duty station for the remainder of his war service. The work camp was turned into a field hospital, treating Allied wounded and camp survivors. It also treated German war prisoners and served as the locale for the trial of collaborators accused of war crimes.

History is nothing if not filled with irony. Not only had the German captors become the captives, Landsberg is the site of Hitler's post-World War I imprisonment. When American forces captured it in 1945, an Army colonel found a plaque above the door to one of the cells that read:

> Here, a dishonorable system imprisoned Germany's greatest son from November 11, 1923 to December 20, 1924. During this time, Adolf Hitler wrote the book of the National Socialist Revolution, *Mein Kampf*.[47]

Leo's duties at Landsberg reflected its somewhat contradictory mission of treating camp victims, Allied and German war wounded, and dealing with German civilians accused of war crimes. It was not unusual for Leo to be asked, after a day of nursing the camp victims and war wounded, to "officiate" at what he recalls being labeled a "legal hanging." A typical charge: pitchforking to death American paratroopers whose lines had become entangled in trees. Leo's job was to declare the death of the person just hanged.

There was a shortage of penicillin at this time, and another of Leo's duties was to certify whether German prisoners of war truly needed the antibiotic. Some of these soldiers were former SS officers. "These were some of the most attentive, compliant patients I ever saw," says Leo. "I swear I could hear their heels click under the sheets as I did my rounds." These patients were, of course, men who would have gladly killed him only weeks earlier.

If he had mixed emotions about treating German POWs, he had only sympathy for the camp victims. "They were so weak they could not walk or take in food; we had to feed them intravenously." He would walk by their beds at night. Often a hand would rise up to touch his arm. A tug, a tap, a stroke. They could not or would not speak. He had to appear strong. He was, after all, the healer, the supposedly dispassionate dispenser of comfort. But it was all he could do to contain himself. These could have been his parents, his brother and sisters. There were times he could not contain himself; he would slip outside to the back of the camp hospital and, where no one could see, put his face in his hands and sob.

On April 30, 1945, with Russian soldiers within a block of his Berlin bunker, Adolf Hitler, the self-proclaimed Fuhrer of the Third Reich and former prisoner of Landsberg, committed suicide. The war was over. On May 6, 1945, just two days after Leo's twenty-seventh birthday, German forces formally surrendered. Victory in Europe, V-E Day, was here at last. Leo still remembers the celebration: "It was quite a party. The Russians even brought vodka; God, could they drink."

In early August came the other news he had been waiting for. He was a father—a baby girl named Phyllis Ann, a combination of the names of one of Lois's closest friends and Leo's sister, was born. He was so ecstatic that he had her name painted on his Jeep for all to see. He spent his spare time searching for handmade dolls to ship back to South Carolina. Each small Czech and German town would have a "Pugelmacher" (doll maker), and Leo would see if the doll maker was available and had dolls to sell. His driver would take him into each of the Occupation Zones as part of the great doll search. Most trips were uneventful, but on one visit to the French Zone, he was stopped and questioned by French soldiers. Certain he was a smuggler or thief, they refused to accept his explanation for the several dolls in his Jeep. While they were considering whether to slice up the dolls, Leo remembered there was a hospital nearby that could X-ray the dolls. The group trundled off to the hospital and, with curious staff looking on, watched as the dolls were examined for contraband.

American soldiers were under standing orders at this time to visit at least one of the actual extermination camps. Each soldier was given official duty time for their visit. "I don't want some son-of-a-bitch fifty years from now saying this didn't happen," General Patton is reported to have said. Leo was not particularly anxious to make the trip. He had, after all, already seen the victims of one camp. But General Patton had ordered it, and that was the end of the discussion.

And so, in the late summer of 1945, Captain Leo Lewis drove in his Jeep—the *Phyllis Ann*—to Munich and then to Dachau.[48] He went with another doctor, Sol Koralek. Both were young Jewish men in their twenties. They had not only heard the stories of the death camps, but they had also met the survivors of the Landsberg work camp. They were also trained wartime physicians—used to the sight of death and human suffering. But nothing could have prepared them for what they saw. They walked by open trenches where bodies had been dumped—fresh with the stench of death. They peered into gas chambers where individuals had been slaughtered because of the

100

accident of their birth and the way in which they chose to worship. Slowly, the sheer enormity of what had happened at this awful place began to sink in. Captain Lewis and Lieutenant Koralek wanted to get away as quickly as they could.

Toward the end of his tour of duty, Babe and Sam wrote him that his mother was ill. He must have sensed that he would not see her again. Leo was not a great letter writer, but now he had to be. In a long letter full of love and admiration, he wrote his "Ma" the following:

> I wish I could see you again. I would like to see you. Can't help missing your family I guess. We have all been through so much together and particularly you. But you have made an accomplishment of your family considering your circum- stances and we all realize it. That is why I would like to see you happy now.

He would never see his mother again. He made a mental note to ask Lois to name a second daughter after her. It also did not escape Leo's thoughts that, had his mother not immigrated to America, she might have been among the six million systematically executed by the Nazi regime. She had a hard life, but one filled with not only the rewards of a loving and close-knit family, but also neighbors who cared. While the Mussolini government in Italy was signing alliances with Hitler and enacting sweeping anti-Semitic laws, her Italian American neighbors were knocking on the wall and deliver- ing hot meals.

The end of the war in Europe turned Leo's thoughts to home. The Army established a system to determine the order of rotation back to the United States. Soon, Leo had enough points to qualify. On the hospital ship *Zebulon B. Price*, he sailed out of Bremen, Germany, and to New York. He cried when he saw the Statue of Liberty, the sight his father and mother must have seen as they approached Ellis Island and a new life. Leo was home, away from the horrors of war and its gruesome reminders. A train ride—"through more tunnels than I had ever seen in my life"—and he was in South Carolina to see Lois and his new daughter. Phyllis had no idea who this strange man was and shied away at first. "She had terrific spunk," Leo remembers. "A lot like my sister Lil."

Back to Chicago for a homecoming with his family, Leo was driven by brother-in-law Sam Solomon to the Great Lakes Naval Station, where he checked out of the Army for the last time. The three of them—Leo, Lois, and Phyllis—lived with Sam and his wife, Edna. Chicago was still on a wartime footing and housing was difficult if not impossible to find. In an attempt to convince Sam's wary landlord to allow them to stay, he and Sam hit on the idea of offering free medical advice. The landlord wasn't buying: "I've already got two doctors; what I'm looking for is a good dentist."

This was not the greatest of living accommodations for either of the young Lewis families, so Leo was on the lookout for job opportunities that might provide housing. One day he was reading a medical journal and saw an ad: "Doctors urgently needed for the U.S. Indian Health Service." Because the headquarters of the Indian Health Service was in Chicago at the Merchandise Mart, Leo went there instead of sending an application through the mail. Delighted to see him, they showed him a book with descriptions and some photographs of various places where the Service needed doctors. As he turned the pages, Leo saw a photo of a beautiful little house in Whiteriver, Arizona. "What about this one?" he asked, only to be told that there was already a doctor there. He did not want to go to Montana or the Dakotas and told them that. They checked again, and it turned out the doctor in Whiteriver was due for a promotion and reassignment to Cherokee, North Carolina.

Leo went home to talk to Lois about the opportunity in a place neither of them had ever been near. When told a house went with the deal, Lois announced she would happily live in a teepee if it would get her out of the crowded apartment they were sharing.

The former newspaper boy was soon back at Union Station, this time loading his family and all their possessions on a Santa Fe train. After a long and tiring trip, they arrived in Holbrook, Arizona. Lois must have wondered if she had spoken too soon about where she would be willing to live. Not only did it look like the face of the moon, but one of the most visible landmarks was a motel with individual units shaped like large teepees. They loaded onto a bus called the "White Mountain Taxi" and headed for the White Mountain Apache Indian Reservation and their new home.

Leo's apprehensions that all this might be too much of an adventure for Lois were short-lived. "She loved the place, especially having a house of her own and a big yard for Phyllis to play in." Leo didn't remember much of what his mother had read him from the Bible in his youth, but he did think about the passage about Ruth: "Whither thou goest, I will go. Whither thou lodgest, I will lodge. Thy people shall be my people. Thy God shall be my God."[49]

Leo and family were at Whiteriver for a little more than one year. While there, he met a pharmaceutical salesman working for the Upjohn Company. His name was Roswell Olsen, and Leo took an instant liking to the tall, affable redhead. They struck up a friendship that would last almost fifty years. It was Roswell who told Leo Lewis about the availability of a job with the Santa Fe Railroad in Winslow. Roswell and his wife, Anne, who had met in a tuberculosis sanitarium in Chicago, were constant visitors to the Lewis home.[50]

Leo, Lois, and Phyllis arrived in Winslow in 1947, eight years after Bert, Pat, and Barry Hawkins. He and his partner, Harry Beckwith—with whom he had something of a tempestuous relationship[51]—practiced medicine in a clinic that was part of La Posada building in Winslow. The building, built in 1929 to serve passengers on the Santa Fe Railroad as a Fred Harvey Hospitality House, is now restored as a hotel and is on the Register of National Historic Landmarks.[52]

With a family that would expand to four children, Leo had a new home. Far from the streets of Chicago, and still farther from the awful memories of a continent gone mad with hatred, his family would make this small town their home for nearly thirty years. He delivered the town's babies (including Mary Patricia Hawkins), fixed their broken limbs (like the time I jumped off the garage and landed on a shovel), and listened to their complaints. Most of them had not seen life from the perspective of someone who had sold newspapers on Chicago's cold streets or walked through a camp fresh with the stench of death. He was just as happy they hadn't.

In his sixties, Leo returned to Flournoy Street. The house was still there and not a bit larger. "You could almost put your nose on the front door, extend your arms out, and touch both sides of the house." He looked for the fireplug, the one near Taglia's Grocery, where Flournoy meets Loomis Street. He found the fireplug that had caused him so much trouble fifty years earlier. Lois was gone now, and all the children were grown and on their own. Reflecting back on a life that had taken him from the mean streets of 1920 Chicago to Hitler's death camps and back, he felt the return of the same feeling that had rushed over him just before he left for Europe. He thought just how fortunate he had been.

The following story has no known connection to Winslow except that Globe, a small town in which the protagonist of the story spent his early professional years, was dominated by a single industry. In Globe, it was mining; in Winslow, it was the railroad.

BLAZING BRIEFCASES

The Amazing Life of Jacob Weinberger, The Longest Surviving Delegate to the 1910 Arizona Constitutional Convention

Federal judges, let alone those from California, are not often invited to address the Arizona Legislature. However, on February 14, 1962, the fiftieth anniversary of Arizona statehood, Senior U.S. District Judge Jacob Weinberger of San Diego returned to Phoenix to share his memories as a delegate to the 1910 proceedings, which set Arizona on the path to statehood. The other delegates had been bankers, mine owners, and cattlemen (there were no women) and included what would become some of the most recognizable names in Arizona history—Hunt, Goldwater, Tovrea, and Osborn. Yet, Jake Weinberger outlived them all. How he got there and what he did there is worth the telling.

From Europe to the New World

Herman Weinberger, Jacob's father, was the son and grandson of Orthodox rabbis. In the mid-1800s, the family was actually quite wealthy. One grandfather, Reb (short for Rabbi) Moshe Wolf, was a published Talmudic scholar and an astute businessman, who married well and prospered. In 1848, all that came to an end as Russian troops, at the urging of Austrian Emperor Franz Joseph, leveled a swath of land and with it the family's home and property.

Life was better for the family by the late 1800s. Herman became a brewer and distiller, accumulating a modest estate. But a fierce anti-Semitism lurked just beneath the surface of everyday life in the Weinberger home near Hedri, Hungary. Funerals and religious ceremonies were held at night for fear of harassment or worse. Political instability, fueled by the territorial ambitions of Hungary's neighbors, led Herman to consider following his brothers to America. In 1886, with their financial help, Herman came to America. His wife, Nettie, and eight children followed three years later. Jacob was all of eight years when the family traveled by train to Hamburg, Germany, and, after a rough sea passage, to Castle Garden, New York, the predecessor to Ellis Island. This would not be their last stop, for the father had set his sights farther west, specifically Colorado.

Denver

The Weinbergers certainly found a more open environment in their new home, but this was, after all, the Wild West. Denver, like San Francisco and other boom towns, was not a place for the faint of heart. Working his way through school as a newspaper boy, young Jacob witnessed an angry mob storm the local jail and lynch a saloonkeeper accused of killing a Civil War veteran.

Through a variety of part-time jobs, including work in the family store, Jake helped put himself through high school,[53] where he excelled in debate and was identified as a young orator who would someday be heard in the halls of Congress.[54] Jacob entered law school at the University of Colorado in 1901, without having first attended college. He worked constantly. During the school year he worked as a waiter at a women's boardinghouse and a janitor at the men's dorm, and in the summer, he worked at a steelworks in Pueblo, where he was paid $1.50 for a day that ran from 7:00 a.m. to 6:00 p.m.

After graduating and passing the bar in the summer of 1904, Jacob tried the practice of law in Denver but found that the doors of downtown law firms and the referrals that might come from them simply were not open to someone of his background. He was accustomed to working hard and producing quality work, but this felt like it was going nowhere. The resulting frustration was broken by a letter from one of his law school classmates, Fred Jeremiah (Jerry) Elliot, who had ventured south to Arizona Territory and was effusive about the opportunities. The copper mining industry was booming, and the resident legal talent in the area was busy looking after the interests of mine owners and no one cared who you were or where you came from. Jacob needed little persuasion; he was headed south.

Globe

All of twenty-three years and with $30 in his pocket, Jacob Weinberger headed to meet up with his buddy. He wasted no time getting started. Literally practicing law by the seat of his pants, he found himself in the mining camps in and around Globe, where Mexican and Cornish mine workers labored by day and filled its never-closing saloons at night, where the City Council had to be told that it had no authority to regulate (and thereby encourage) prostitution.

Jacob's legal skills were both apparent and quickly recognized. Seeing a fresh face among the lawyers in his court, a local judge appointed Jake to defend a young indigent man from Mexico accused of killing the popular sheriff's equally popular brother-in-law. Putting his heart and soul into the defense, Jake was able to spare his client the gallows and, when it was established that another man was responsible, secure the man's release. The grateful client, in no position to pay, instead rewarded Jacob with a stuffed Gila monster.[55] After just two years, County Attorney Fred Shute invited Jake to become one of his part-time deputies.[56] Along with Jerry Elliot, they split their days, working in the morning for the County and the afternoon for private clients. Jake found criminal defendants not as warmhearted when he prosecuted; one left the courtroom swearing to kill every trial participant, the judge and Jake included. Fortunately, the man ran into a deputy sheriff at a local watering hole first. The ensuing gunfight earned the man a sufficiently long prison stretch to put Jake out of harm's way.[57]

Young Weinberger made friends easily. One of his earliest friends in Globe was a local businessman and banker, George W.P. Hunt, who would become the president of the Constitutional Convention and later the seven-term governor of Arizona. Another friend, Max Lantin, who owned a local clothing store, introduced Jacob to his sister-in-law, Blanche Ruth Solomon. Blanche was the daughter of a prominent banking and mercantile family that had founded Solomonville, a town ninety miles east of Globe.[58] The wedding ceremony, presided over by Rabbi Martin Zielonka of El Paso, was reported in detail in the local newspaper.[59] The marriage would last sixty-one years.

The Delegate

There was an early effort to bring New Mexico and Arizona Territories into the Union as one state, a proposal widely opposed in Arizona. Jacob, whose high school debating skills had not left him, was among those speaking out against the idea. When the New Mexico idea faded and Congress passed the June 1910 Enabling Act, allowing the election of delegates in Arizona to frame a constitution, young Weinberger became a candidate. He was, by this time, reasonably well known and respected in Globe and the surrounding mining camps; and the support of friends like George Hunt did not hurt.

On September 12, 1910, Jacob Weinberger, now twenty-eight, became one of five delegates elected from Gila County.[60] He had more miles to travel, and they would not be easy. Few paved roads existed on the trek from Globe to Phoenix, and Jake would later remember the trip vividly:

> I will never forget the trip coming down the narrow winding unpaved road, down steep grades and sharp, hair-pin turns. We made the trip in one of the early makes of automobiles, that had no fringe on top, an uncovered wagon as it were, and we used an umbrella at times when needed for shade.[61]

Paid the princely sum of $6 per day, the delegates were required to complete their work in sixty days. It took sixty-one, Jacob recalled in 1963: "We had to turn back the clock twenty-four hours to get the job done on time."[62]

The Convention

Fifty-two delegates gathered at the Capitol building on October 19, 1910, to be sworn in as delegates by Chief Justice Kent of the Territorial Supreme Court. Fourteen of the delegates were, like Jacob, lawyers. There were cattlemen, sheepmen, merchants, railroaders, bankers, and one (M.G. Cunniff of Prescott) self-described capitalist, but no women. Their first act was to elect Judge A.C. Baker from Phoenix as the temporary chair, who then called the Convention to order. George W.P. Hunt, Jacob's friend from Globe, was elected as president and Morris Goldwater, of Prescott, as vice president.

Jacob genuinely admired Hunt. Although a large (six feet tall, over three hundred pounds) and physically imposing man with a shaved head and walrus mustache, Hunt was soft spoken, friendly, and cultured. As the presiding officer of the Convention, Jake thought he conducted the sessions with order and dignity, seldom taking to the floor to participate in the debate and always considerate of the views of others.[63] He had similar admiration for Morris Goldwater, although the two had not met before the Convention. He thought Goldwater was successful in straightening out misunderstandings with his good sense of humor and practical ideas. He kept the machinery of the Convention operating smoothly, Jake would later recall.[64] The six-term mayor of Prescott, unlike his nephew Barry, was, like a majority of the delegates, a Democrat. Fifty years later, when Senator Barry Goldwater invited Jake to attend a dinner marking the occasion, Jake brought the house down with this line: "If we Democrats at the Convention in 1910 had known that Arizona would ever go Republican, we would have never formed the state."[65]

Jacob was impressed by the lawyer-delegates. Judge A.C. Baker from Maricopa County brought considerable prior government experience, and, as a former chief justice of the Territorial Supreme Court, he had been a county prosecutor and had served as Phoenix city attorney. Lysander Cassidy, also from Maricopa County, displayed clear logic in his arguments, while maintaining a modest and reserved demeanor. Jacob recalls Cassidy securing passage of a measure calling for legislators to be paid $6 per day, with a deduction of $5 if the member failed to vote on roll call. The proposal, as might be expected, did not pass.[66] E.E. Ellinwood of Cochise County, a U.S. attorney in territorial days, participated in some of the most spirited debates of the Convention.

A first order of business was to set up committees to produce proposals for inclusion in the new constitution. Twenty-one committees were formed, each with a chairman and from three to thirteen members. Jacob Weinberger found himself on four committees (and what a four they were): Legislative Department, Distribution of Powers & Apportionment, Executive, and Impeachment & Removal (which he chaired). His friend George Hunt saw to it that Jake was also put on the committee on Style, Revision & Compilation, the Arizona equivalent of being on the Committee on Detail at the Philadelphia Convention in 1787. Jacob worked there with its chair, M.G. Cunniff of Yavapai County. Boston born, Harvard educated, and a serious student of the English language, Cunniff taught Jacob more about grammar and sentence structure than he ever learned in school.

A theme that permeated the deliberations, a fear of entrenched power, showed up in the deliberations of the Committee on Impeachment & Removal, the committee Jacob chaired. It produced the single most controversial proposal of the Convention, one that almost derailed statehood: recall of judges. In the midst of the debate over the issue, President William Howard Taft made clear he would veto any creation of legislation that included recall of judges. The debate produced such acrimony that ten of the eleven Republican delegates refused to sign the proposed constitution (only John Langdon, Jake's fellow delegate from Gila County, signed). Jake, Hunt, Goldwater, and Ellinwood were among the forty-one Democratic delegates who unanimously approved the final draft.[67] In the end, the Convention thought discretion (or perhaps delay) was the better part of valor and removed the offending provision, only to promptly put it back after statehood was achieved.

Moving On

For all his efforts at the very creation of the forty-eighth state, Jacob Weinberger would not be around on February 14, 1912, when Arizona officially joined the union. In 1911, he packed up his family and headed to San Diego, a place now so frequently visited by Arizonans in the summer months that the locals have a name for them: "Zonies." But Jake's move was not temporary; San Diego would become his home for the rest of his years. Why he left is not entirely clear. When asked about it some years later, he would cite the health of his wife, Blanche. In other interviews, he suggested that Globe's dependence on a single industry worried him. The demand for copper could slacken and labor troubles could turn the citizens of mining communities against one another. This, of course, is exactly what happened five years into statehood, producing the Bisbee Deportation of 1917, one of the darkest days in Arizona history.[68]

The man who had come to Globe with $30 in his pocket left with $30,000, the product of a wise investment in a mining venture. And just as he had in Globe, Jake folded into life in San Diego, a community large enough to have a synagogue where the family could worship, without exporting a rabbi from El Paso. He opened a law office and later established a law firm that exists to this day. His mining camp courtroom exploits behind him, Jake was now a business lawyer, with a reputation as a shrewd negotiator, providing, in the words of a colleague, "astute, sagacious advice in both law and politics."[69] He was most proud of his lengthy service on the San Diego Board of Education, and an elementary school bears his name.

In 1941, Jake became the city attorney of San Diego, serving there for two years. His young delegate views that judges should be accountable to the voting public came home to roost. After being appointed to the Superior Court, he had to stand for election, and, in 1945, became the first San Diego judge unseated by election.[70] There was something of a consolation prize: On February 21, 1946, having been nominated by President Truman, Jacob Weinberger was commissioned as a United States District Judge for the Southern District of California. He took senior status in 1958 but continued to hear cases. One of his favorite duties was to preside over naturalization ceremonies, where he estimated that he gave the oath to some 16,000 new citizens. He knew something about being an immigrant, and the words he often used to close the ceremony reflected a deep patriotism, born of the opportunities given to him by his adopted country: "Give America your best and she will return it three-fold."

Twenty years after his passing, a large crowd gathered outside the San Diego courthouse where Judge Weinberger served. The building had sat empty for years but was now restored to its original luster. The Marine Corps Band was present, along with members of the Weinberger family and students from the Weinberger Elementary

School. The chiseled words above the entrance told why the crowd was there that day: "The Jacob Weinberger United States Courthouse." As you would expect, the flags of the United States and California were prominently displayed. But to the side of the podium was another flag, one with a copper star in the middle and a blazing sunset above a pure blue sky. It was the flag of Arizona. A fitting end to the long journey of one remarkable man.

ENDNOTES

Endnotes for The People v. Uncle Winnie

1 During the 1960 presidential campaign, Senator John F. Kennedy's staff would wile away their downtime by playing what they called the "Question Game" in which one person would come up with an answer and challenge the others to come up with a question, making sense of the combination. On Election Day three of JFK's staffers (Richard Goodwin, Mike Feldman, and Theodore Sorensen) came up with this challenge answer: "Nine W." After trying various alternatives, one of them found the question: "Do you spell your name with a 'V,' Herr Wagner?" Theodore H. White, *The Making of the President 1960*, paperback edition, 2009, 284.

2 *The Coconino Sun*, March 7, 1907.

3 Earle R. Forrest, "War With the Rustlers," 12 *Frontier Times*, 1935, 258-60.

4 This was confirmed by the findings of the coroner's inquest as reported in the March 7, 1907 *Coconino Sun*: "The evidence given before the [coroner's] jury went to show that the witnesses had just entered the back door to the house, but none of them remained to see the shot fired. All, however, say that they believed it was a race for guns, and that 'business was meant' so they got to cover as quickly as they could."

5 George Hochderffer, *Flagstaff Whoa! The Autobiography of a Western Pioneer*, Northland Press, 1965, 123-24.

6 *Coconino Sun*, February 28, 1997.

7   *The Territory of Arizona v. H.V. Rosenberger*, No. 773. District Court for the Fourth Judicial District of the Territory of Arizona, in and for the County of Yavapai. (Records of the Arizona State Archives.)

8   *Frontier Times*, supra, 1935, 259-60. For a description of the Graham-Tewksbury feud and the resulting trial of Ed Tewksbury, see Don Dedera, *A Little War of our Own: The Pleasant Valley Feud Revisited* (1988), 239-50.

9   Judge Sloan presided over the 1884 criminal trial of several Solomonville men for the robbery of a payroll detachment under the command of U.S. Army Major James W. Wham. The event became known as the Wham Robbery. See "The Politics and Personalities of Arizona's Quest for Statehood 1890-1912," 26 *Western Legal History* 4-5 (2013).

10   Because of the outcome of the trial, there is no actual transcript of the proceedings. Instead, we rely on the writings of newspaper reporters covering the trial. It is hard to imagine, however, that Winnie's counsel did not ask Bailey if he could tell whether it was an entry or exit wound.

11   Some twenty years later, James L. Black was convicted of manslaughter for the July 28, 1928, murder of Charles B. Otey and sentenced to 9-10 years in prison. "War With the Rustlers" at 260. On September 27, 1957, Arizona Governor Raleigh C. Stanford granted Black a full and unconditional pardon. Records of the Arizona State Archives.

12   *Coconino Sun*, March 14, 1907, 1.

13   A leather sheath or holster for holding a handgun.

14   The coroner's jury consisted of: School Principal Benjamin H. Shudder (foreman), businessman Charles R. Hooker, Deputy Sheriff W.S. Owen, Jerome Town Marshal Fred Hawkins, merchant W.P. Scott, and local bank employee Guy Bailey. The jury conducted its inquiry at the Windmill Ranch. *Coconino Sun*, March 7 and 14, 1907.

15   Ibid., 260.

Endnotes for Line of Duty

16 *Lawrence v. State*, 240 P. 863 (1925).

17 *The Arizona Republican* of March 26, 1925, identifies the members of Will Lawrence's jury: George B. Hodgson, Julian Powers, T.W. Jones, R. Brimhall, E.J. Harrington, Oscar F. Harrison, Frank Irving, Joe Connor, Andy Treats, V.W. Wheat, William H. Perry and Charles Weeks. That William K. Perry was sitting in for his father was apparently of little note.

Endnotes for The Winslow Boys

18 Richard Kleindienst, *Justice: The Memoirs of an Attorney General*, Jameson Books (Ottawa, Illinois 1985) (*"Kleindienst Memoirs"*), 7-8.

19 I had occasion, following Bill Mahoney's death, to read some of his journal entries. He was an unusually gifted writer. One of his favorite journal entries, written September 1942, appears at the front of this story.

20 Wm. P. Mahoney, Jr., *Son of an Immigrant: The Memoirs of William P. Mahoney, Jr.*, Burrishoole Press (Phoenix, Arizona 1995) (*"Mahoney Memoirs"*), 22.

21 *Mahoney Memoirs*, 40.

22 Several years after first writing this story, while serving as the Editor of *Western Legal History*, our Book Review Editor suggested we review *Judgment at Tokyo: The Japanese War Crime Trials* (2023). I sought out Bill Mahoney's son, Richard Mahoney, now teaching history at North Carolina State University, and he kindly agreed to write the review.

23 Bill Mahoney learned something about honor in the process. Admiral Abe identified a Captain Hayashi as the officer who was at the scene of the execution and gave the order to proceed. When a story appeared in the *Stars & Stripes* about Abe's trial, Captain

Hayashi appeared in Mahoney's office and freely admitted his actions. Taken aback by his forthrightness, Mahoney acceded to Hayashi's request to return to his home to say a last farewell to his family. True to his word, Captain Hayashi returned to Mahoney's office one week later to face eventual trial and execution. *Mahoney Memoirs*, 95-96.

24 Patrick James Fitzgerald, Bill Mahoney's grandfather, came from Cork, Ireland, at the age of 25 and first worked as a miner in the Turkey Creek-Crown King area in the Bradshaw Mountains south of Prescott. *Mahoney Memoirs*, 5. He would have arrived in Arizona Territory at about the same time as my great-grandfather, William Henry Perry, and his Dublin-born wife, Mary Agnes Clark Perry.

25 Tom Tang became a long-time law partner of Bill Mahoney's and went on to become a superior court judge in Phoenix and president of the State Bar of Arizona, the first Asian-American to hold either post. In 1978, he was appointed to the U.S. Court of Appeals for the Ninth Circuit. When he took senior status in 1993, I had the honor of filling the resulting vacancy. Tom Tang was surely one of the most decent people I have ever known. We lost him in 1995.

26 Along with Phoenix lawyers Herb Finn and Hayzel Daniels, Bill had successfully pursued a state court action resulting in a 1953 determination that the practice was unconstitutional. This was one year prior to the landmark decision by the United States Supreme Court in *Brown v. Board of Education*, 347 U.S. 483 (1954).

27 Mahoney did not endear himself to the newspaper and its friends any further when he later went after bingo games being operated at the Camelback Inn in a suburb of Phoenix. The then-owner of the Inn, a powerful member of the local establishment and an equally well-known anti-Semite, called Mahoney and threatened him with political retribution. Herb Caen, the Pultizer Prize-winning columnist for *The San Francisco Chronicle*, later wrote a column about the incident entitled, "No Room at the Inn."

28 *Kleindienst Memoirs*, 21.

29 The managing editor of *The Arizona Republic* at the time was the father of future Vice President Dan Quayle. The elder Quayle would later be "horrified" by what he believed was the unfair treatment of his son by the press.

30 Among them: Congressman Stewart Udall, who went on to become Secretary of the Interior; his brother Morris K. "Mo" Udall, who served in Congress for many years and, despite the title of his book, *Too Funny to be President*, was a serious Presidential candidate in 1976; and Carl Muecke, who would become U.S. Attorney for Arizona and later a U.S. District Court Judge that *The Arizona Republic* loved to hate as much as they had Bill Mahoney.

31 Mecham would later win the governor's chair, only to be impeached and removed from office. Sam Goddard's son, former Phoenix Mayor Terry Goddard, twice ran for governor himself.

32 Bill's son Richard, who served as Secretary of State (essentially Lt. Governor) of Arizona (1990-1994), has written a wonderful book on the subject. Richard Mahoney, *JFK: Ordeal in Africa*, Harcourt Brace (1994).

33 *Kleindienst Memoirs*, 22.

34 The federal judge who sentenced Richard Kleindienst described his violation as not being "the type that reflects a mind bent on deception; rather it reflects a heart that is too loyal and considerate of the feelings of others." *Kleindienst Memoirs*, 175-76.

35 When Dennis DeConcini began his race for the Senate, there was a campaign kickoff event in Phoenix. As Bill Mahoney introduced Dennis to a crowd of mostly lawyers, I couldn't help but think that maybe deep down he might have wished it was about ten years earlier and that he was the candidate. One of Dennis's first staff hires was Mary Mahoney, Bill and Alice Mahoney's daughter. Mary served 18 years in the Senator's office and was widely admired for her quick wit and friendly can-do attitude.

36 Richard joked that there were four "tribes" in Winslow: the Navajos, the Hopis, the Kleindiensts and the Mahoneys.

Endnotes for Going Home

37 "Take It Easy," Jackson Browne and Glenn Frey (1972) (Copyright Warner Bros. Music Corp. and Red Cloud Music).

38 No true-blooded person from Winslow would ever knowingly give credit to an eagle, the mascot of Flagstaff High School. True, the song "Take it Easy" was made famous by the Eagles, but the line about Winslow was written by Jackson Browne, who co-authored the lyrics with Glen Frey. Besides, the Eagles once had the effrontery to modify the lyrics to say, "Standing on a corner in Southern California."

Endnotes for The Flournoy Fireplug

39 Just after the 1918 World Series, the Red Sox traded a left-handed pitcher by the name of Babe Ruth to the New York Yankees. The Cubs would endure an even longer drought after winning the Series in 1908—108 years.

40 Margaret Sanger (1879-1966) had begun speaking out on the issue in 1912 but had to flee to Europe in 1914 when a pamphlet containing explicit instructions for contraception was confiscated by U.S. Post authorities and a warrant was issued for her arrest. Returning to the United States in 1915, she and her sister Evelyn Byrn established the nation's first birth control clinic in Brooklyn. Eric Foner and John A. Garraty, *The Reader's Companion to American History* (Houghton Mifflin, 1991), 963.

41 It is a testament to the futility of enforcing Prohibition that Abraham Lewis, grandfather of Phyllis Hawkins, and Frank Daly, grandfather of Michael Hawkins, although miles and cultures apart, both had stills. See "The Search of Effie Dee".

42 His friend may not have realized it, but at about this time Jewish doctors were barred from practicing medicine in German institutions. Simon Wiesenthal Center, *"Timeline of the Holocaust 1938-1945"* www.wiesenthal.com/resource/timeline/html.

43 For World War II history, I rely heavily on two fine books by Stephen E. Ambrose, the imminent World War II historian, for the military and historical context: *"Citizen Soldiers: The U.S. Army from the Normandy Beaches to the Bulge to the Surrender of Germany"* (Simon & Schuster 1997) and *"The Victors: Eisenhower and His Boys: The Men of World War II"* (Simon & Schuster 1998) and on Martin Gilbert's massive one-volume *"The Second World War: A Complete History"* (Henry Holt & Co. Rev. Edit. 1991).

44 Ambrose, *Citizen Soldier*, 321. Out of the assembly line triage that characterized field hospitals come some wonderful stories. One Red Cross nurse, reading the chart to determine the extent of one soldier's injuries asked: "How on earth did you get shot with two arrows?" The Native American on the cot allowed as how that was his name, not a description of his injuries. Ibid., 325.

45 Ambrose, *The Victors* at 337. As bad as Landsberg was, it pales in comparison to the death camp just a few miles away at Dachau. On April 27, 1945, as elements of the U.S. 12th Armored Division approached the camp, they saw an acrid smoke coming from the camp's outskirts. The SS officer in charge had ordered some four thousand slave laborers inside their wooden barracks, hosed the buildings down with gasoline, and set them ablaze. Ibid., 342.

46 Ibid., 337.

47 Gilbert, 674. Landsberg Prison was also the site of several War Crimes Trials, including those of Oswald Pohl (in charge of goods and chattels of murdered camp victims), Otto Ohlendorf (commander of special killing squads in German-occupied Russia) and Wernher Braune (another special killing squad commander). Ibid., 735.

48 Dachau was among the worst of the death camps. From the earliest days of the War, it housed prisoners of conscience, faith, and race. On September 9, 1939, one week after the invasion of Poland, some 630 Czech political prisoners were sent there. One of Hitler's would-be assassins was sent and murdered there; many of the worst medical experiments went on there; in November 1940, 55 Polish intellectuals became the victims of the first mass execution there; Russian, British, and Allied officers were executed there; and, of course, thousands of European Jews, Gypsies, and other "enemies of Germany" died there. Some 300,000 men, women, and children went into Dachau. When Allied troops captured it on April 28, 1945, there were some 30,000 survivors (2,500 of whom died in the next month). Gilbert, 7, 496, 585, 660, 668-78.

49 King James version, Book of Ruth 1:16.

50 It is truly a small world. One of Roswell and Anne Olsen's daughters, Roslyn (now Roslyn Silver), and I went to law school together and practiced together in a small firm and in the U.S. Attorney's office in Phoenix. A childhood playmate of Phyllis's, Roslyn is now a U.S. District Judge—the first woman to be a federal trial judge sitting in Phoenix.

51 I can always bring a big smile to Leo's face when taking a photograph by having him say: "I outlived Beckwith."

52 The La Posada was designed by Mary Colter, an architect when few women practiced the profession. She designed a series of Harvey House stops along the Santa Fe route, including the South Rim of the Grand Canyon, the Painted Desert, and Gallup and Albuquerque, New Mexico. S. Spano, "Winslow Inn a Harvey House That Mary Built" *Los Angeles Times*, reprinted in December 5, 1999, T-9. Janice Griffith, a high school classmate of Sarah Lewis's (the second daughter named for Leo's mother), was instrumental in saving La Posada from the wrecking ball.

Endnotes for Blazing Briefcases

53 The first two years were at West Denver High School, the last two in Victor, Colorado, high in the Rocky Mountains near Cripple Creek. Leland G. Stanford *90 Weinberger Years* (Law Library Justice Foundation 1971), 34-37.

54 Ibid., 37.

55 The stuffed lizard remained on Jake's desk through much of his later judicial service as a reminder of the importance of the presumption of innocence. *The San Diego Union World Review*, September 23, 1951, 1.

56 Interview of Judge Jacob Weinberger by Marjorie H. Wilson of the Arizona State University Department of History, January 14, 1971. Archives of the ASU Hayden Library (Weinberger & Ramenofsky Collection MMS-150).

57 *90 Weinberger Years*, 54-55.

58 Solomonville was founded in 1872 by Isidor Elkan Solomon, a Polish immigrant, who established what became the Valley National Bank of Arizona (now, after several acquisitions, Chase Bank of Arizona). *90 Weinberger Years*, 55-58. Also, see, Elizabeth L. Ramenofsky, *From Charcoal to Banking: The I.E. Solomons of Arizona* (Westernlore Press, 1984).

59 *The Arizona Bulletin*, June 14, 1907, quoted verbatim, Ibid., 59-60.

60 The other delegates from Gila County were George W.P. Hunt, saloonkeeper J.J. Keegan, businessman Alfred Kinney, and mechanic John Langdon. All but Langdon were Democrats. Roscoe Wilson, A Lone Survivor of Convention@ *Arizona Republic*, November 5, 1967. The youngest delegate was twenty-seven-year-old Sidney P. Osborn of Maricopa County, who would later become Governor of Arizona. Framer of Arizona Constitution Remembers Bitter Fight, @ *Arizona Daily Star*, February 14, 1963.

61 Jacob Weinberger Remarks to the Arizona Senate, February 14, 1962.

62 *Arizona Daily Star*, February 14, 1963.

63 Jacob Weinberger April 18, 1963, speech on the occasion of the fiftieth anniversary of the creation of Arizona Territory. Files of the Arizona Historical Foundation at Hayden Library, Arizona State University.

64 Ibid.

65 Remarks of Senior U.S. Circuit Judge James Carter at the Memorial Service for Jacob Weinberger, 454 F. Supp. 6 (1978).

66 Jacob Weinberger, Address to the Arizona Senate, February 14, 1962, 10 (Arizona Historical Foundation files, ASU's Hayden Library).

67 Bill Becker, "Framer of Arizona Constitution Remembers Bitter Fight," *Arizona Daily Star*, February 14, 1963.

68 James W. Byrkit, *"Forging the Copper Collar: Arizona's Labor-Management War of 1901-1921," University of Arizona Press*, Tucson, Arizona (2016).

69 Remarks of Judge James Carter at Weinberger Memorial, 454 F. Supp. 7 (1978).

70 Remarks of U.S. District Judge Gordon Thompson, Jr., at Weinberger Memorial, 454 F. Supp. 12 (1978).

www.ingramcontent.com/pod-product-compliance
Lightning Source LLC
Chambersburg PA
CBHW021115130626
46554CB00002B/702